Making A Difference

Making a Difference

When our hearts are open, we readily help others…

WAYNE DOUGLAS HARRISON

Making A Difference

The **Journeys of Courage** series
Making A Difference by Wayne Douglas Harrison
First Edition

Copyright © 2021 Wayne Douglas Harrison
All rights reserved

No part of this series is to be copied or reproduced in any form or by any electronic or mechanical means including information storage and retrieval systems without permission in writing from the author. The only exception is by a reviewer, who may quote short excerpts in review.

This book is a work of fiction. It takes place in the author's hometown of Saint John, New Brunswick, Canada. The characters, their names, and actions are products of the author's imagination and are used fictitiously.
To contact Wayne Douglas Harrison,
authorwaynedouglasharrison@gmail.com
Visit my website: www.authorwaynedouglasharrison.com

Brainspired Publishing
A joint venture of Brainchild Holdings Inc. and INspired Media Inc.
Brainspired Publishing Ontario, Canada
www.brainspiredpublishing.com

PAPERBACK ISBN: 978-1-7779490-8-2

Library and Archives Canada / Government of Canada Tel: 819-953-3997 or 1-866-578-7777

Making A Difference

Other books in the **Journeys of Courage** series include:

Out of Fear (2nd edition 2021)

Into Uncertainty (2nd edition 2021)

Taking Control (2nd edition 2021)

Making A Difference

For my husband, Ross, whose constant support makes my life so much easier.

Making A Difference

The Journeys of Courage series

Making A Difference

Chapter 1

Martha Matheson entered the kitchen and saw, her husband, Grant standing over two unopened boxes, sitting on the table, scanning a piece of paper. "I heard the doorbell and thought it might be Jane. What are those?"

Grant looked up from the newspaper, "According to this letter, these boxes were part of Father Mike's estate and he left instructions in his will that they were to be sent to me."

"But he died two years ago, why are they just arriving now?"

"His lawyers are just now finalizing everything, and the boxes somehow got set aside. They found them and couriered them to me." Grant stopped talking and stood there in a daze.

Martha broke the silence, "Well, let's see what he wanted you to have." She passed him a pair scissors, "Here, use these."

Grant took the scissors but stood, not doing anything.

"Why are you waiting?"

"I'm afraid of what might be in them. When we visited him eight years ago and confronted him about abusing me, he gave me that letter he would have instructed someone to mail after his death. Now this arrives, I can't imagine what it could be."

"Well, let's find out. If you won't open them, I will." Martha said as she took the scissors and sliced through the thick taped edges of both boxes, "OK, they're open, are you ready to look at what's inside? Wait, there's an envelope on the top of this one." She lifted the flap wide open, took the letter out, and handed it to him.

Grant opened it and found one single page which he quickly unfolded. "It's from Father Mike and it's dated January 4, 2022. This had to be written just weeks before he died."

Martha was eager, "I wonder if he knew he was dying? Please, read it out loud."

Dear Grant,

I apologize for the shaky handwriting; I am so drained of all my energy that I can barely hold the pen. Even though I have all three vaccines, I think I have caught the Delta Variant which is running rampant around here since the fourth wave has hit St. John's in December. I have

Making A Difference

decided I need to go to the hospital and get tested. I have put this off much too long, but I need to do this before I go. I may not have another chance.

Grant, this box contains all the information I have gathered about our Church and the effort they have put into hiding the sexual abuse over the years. Much of what I am sending are copies of archived documents that I have chanced upon while in the guise of doing research on other topics. If the powers that be knew, I would not have been able to copy any of the information.

Most of the priests are very old or dead but the big issue is the coverup the Church orchestrated. I am sending it to you because you will know, or find out, how to use it to make a difference in the lives of the abused. I do not hold you to anything so if you choose to do nothing, I understand that is what you need to do. I leave it in your hands.

Your decision not to pursue charging me with your abuse is something I am thankful for even though you had every right to do so. For that reason, I give you this information which is damning against the Church as an institution. If you choose to pursue this, I am listing a few priests who have told me they would help uncover things inside the Church if anyone needed an inside resource.

I'm glad you came to visit me in 2016. I think of it often and it has provided me with a measure of comfort that I never thought I would have or even deserved. You're a good man.

Now to get these boxes taped up and ready for you in case I don't get home again. If I do, I will mail them to you, if not, I have added specific instructions in my will to get them to you.

Take care of yourself and your family.

Love,
Father Mike'

Grant looked at Martha, "He must have tested positive for Covid19 and subsequently died. Let's look at what we have here." He started unpacking the boxes and reviewed what was coming to light as he read the various notes that Father Mike added to each of the documents. The documents covered several areas of the abuse coverup by the Church including lists of priests' names, and the names of abused children.

Martha and Grant stood looking at the piles of documents for several minutes sizing up the magnitude of what they were seeing. They turned to each other, and Grant was the first to speak, "I don't know what to say."

Martha gave him a hug and added, "It looks like you have lots to think about. I thought it was over when you visited him and made up your mind to leave everything be."

Making A Difference

"So, did I. When we heard about his death a couple of years ago, I put the abuse and everything about it to rest. I think I processed it well and I didn't feel like I needed to do anything more, but this adds a whole new dimension to it. This is so much bigger than me. I don't know if it's fair of me to say no and just drop it."

"The Church has been getting so much bad publicity and I'm not saying they don't deserve it. I just find it hard to digest that an organization which is supposed to be a place for people to turn to for comfort can cause so much hurt and emotional damage. What they sanctioned in the Residential Schools is beyond belief. Why would anyone look to the Church for guidance when they make such a mess out of people's lives?" Martha did a slow, mournful shake of her head.

"I want to talk this over with Brock and Mackenzie when they come tomorrow for Family Supper night. Not only are they our children, I also see them as valuable resources who I can count on to be here to discuss issues with when I need a listening ear and a different point of view."

*****

Brock met Mackenzie as he left his home, which was next door to their parents' house. They walked together to the kitchen door and entered to hugs and the smell of their mother's fantastic cooking. They spent the first fifteen minutes or so catching up on everyone's life and then went to work setting the dining table for supper. They each relished these family gatherings and amidst the conversation and laughter they reconnected with each others lives. These family get togethers were started by Grant after a stay in hospital with a health scare several years ago. It was then that he realized life was too short and decided he wanted his family to connect in person at least once a week around their dining table. In the eight years they rarely missed one.

They had progressed through the main course and we're just finishing dessert when Grant spoke about the boxes that Father Mike had earmarked for him. Brock looked interested and Mackenzie was impatient to ask questions but knew she needed to wait to hear all that her father was explaining. When he finished all he knew about the contents of the boxes, he asked, "So, you now know as much as I do. What's going through your minds?"

Mackenzie couldn't wait, "So you've done a cursory inspection, are you planning to look at the contents in more detail?"

Grant looked around the table and responded, "I think that's the next logical step, but there is more than logic connected to the contents of those boxes.

Making A Difference

They document things that are tied to emotions which aren't easy to deal with. This is why I wanted to get your assessment about what to do next."

Brock leaned closer, "We need to do a detailed analysis, so we know exactly what we are dealing with. It sounds like Father Mike organized components, so I'd like to understand what his system was and, from there we should document everything." He stopped and noticed his mother hadn't said a word, "Mom, you have been very quiet about this, what are your thoughts?"

She paused before speaking and was fidgeting with her napkin, "OK, here is where I am. Those boxes are an emotional time bomb. Your father has done a lot of therapy and went out of his way to visit both the Bishop and Father Mike and they're now both dead. I don't know the full extent of what's in the boxes, but I do know that it involves predators who are, most likely, dead, and many victims who are still alive. We were all affected by the depth of the torment your father went through and I can only guess the victims identified in those boxes have been, or are still being, tormented by what the contents represent. If we open this up to an investigation, I'm concerned about where it will go and who it will hurt. If it means that only the church as an organization will be taken to task, I think that would be a good outcome. My concern is about the emotional shrapnel when this explodes because I know it will?"

Martha's points brought the whole issue into perspective. Everyone sat in quiet contemplation of the true meaning of her words.

Brock broke the silence, "Well said, Mom. Whatever we do, we need to be mindful of the collateral damage that could come from it. Having said that, I think we can organize ourselves and determine the options we have. Let's take it one step at a time. I think we really need to understand what those boxes are giving us and once we know that, we can make the decision of doing something or nothing."

Mackenzie nodded, "I agree. We don't have to go beyond the understanding stage for now or ever, if that's where we want to stop."

Martha was thinking about what her kids had said and spoke, "You're right. Let's see this as a puzzle and work to understand all that Father Mike has given us. What do you think Grant?"

"I like that we aren't committing to anything but understanding what we have. I could go along with that. So, now that we agree, what's our next step?"

"We start by categorizing and documenting the contents wouldn't you say?" Mackenzie said as she looked from one to the next around the table.

Brock added, "Yes, and once we have that done, we can look at how Father Mike organized it. He must have a system and we need to decipher what it is. I have

Making A Difference

some free time next Sunday. How about we start just after lunch and work into the afternoon just before our family supper?" He saw all heads nodding. "Then, next Sunday it is. Let's meet here at one o'clock."

Chapter 2

Kaleisha walked into the kitchen, "Good morning! Today is a special day for me; Eight years ago, you hired me as manager of Mahogany Manor!"

Kaleisha brightened any room she walked into with her radiant smile and infectious energy. Today she was overflowing and caused Andrew and Gregory to get up from the table to greet her with a spontaneous group hug, "That makes it a special day for us too, you have made our lives so much better." Gregory said as they hugged and when they parted, he continued, "All of the guests are staying another night so it will be a light day tidying up, but they'll soon be down for breakfast. I'll set the table and you both can start the food." He headed for the dining room.

Andrew started the coffee and began preparing the fruit plates.

Kaleisha had her special French toast cooking on the electric grill and bacon sizzling in the oven when Gregory returned. "There, we're all set. I heard movement from upstairs so they should be down shortly."

The guests filled in the empty seats, and, in quick succession, the table was full. Andrew served the fruit plates while Gregory poured coffee all the while chatting and getting an idea of what each guest needed to help plan their day. By the time breakfast was over, the guests had dispersed except the last two who were getting maps and information from Kaleisha.

When she returned to the kitchen, she heard the front door open and close and thought the guests were letting themselves out for the day. She heard footsteps approaching and looked up to see her life partner, Roger, enter the kitchen, rush over to her, pick her up, and swing her around. "Woman, I've missed you so much!" They kissed, hugged, and then realized that they weren't alone. Andrew and Gregory had entered just after Roger and witnessed the affection they had for each other.

Kaleisha was trying to manage her blushing and spoke, "Sorry but he's been away for three days and I'm just so happy to see him."

Gregory tried to relieve her concern, "Don't ever be embarrassed by love. You thought you were alone." He looked to Roger, "We haven't seen you for a while. Kaleisha told us you had to help your mother move into a senior's apartment complex."

"Yes, she set it all up by herself without telling anyone until she needed help moving. Several of her friends have moved into the same complex, so I think they helped convince her. She found the responsibility of looking after the homestead since Dad died was just too much. She has a small apartment in a senior's complex that will look after her needs as her abilities decline. One stop shopping!"

Andrew smiled, "Why don't you both take a couple of hours. The load is light today, and we can manage while you're out."

"Thank you, I'll take my lunch break now and be back to get my work done."

They walked off holding hands. The guys smiled and watched as they disappeared, "It's hard to believe they have been together about three years now. I'm so glad they found each other."

*****

Andrew and Gregory were sitting at the kitchen table when Kaleisha returned. Andrew patted the seat next to him, "Welcome back. Come sit down, we have something we want to discuss with you."

Kaleisha's face paled and her radiant smile was replaced with concern. As she took her seat, she cautioned, "What have I done?"

"Nothing but the best job we could ask of anyone. We're thinking of selling Mahogany Manor and would like to offer you the opportunity to be the new owner."

Kaleisha sat back and exhaled in a long slow breath. Her eyes were unfocused staring straight ahead not really looking at anything. The guys knew she needed time and they sat, allowing her to process what Andrew had said. When she spoke, she relayed her concerns, "I'd love to own Mahogany Manor Bed and Breakfast, but I don't know how I could possibly afford it. I do have some money saved from my late husband's insurance and I could sell my home, but I don't think I could get a mortgage for the rest."

Gregory saw the turmoil they had caused and spoke to reassure her. "We assumed that you might not have the money readily available, so we're prepared to hold the mortgage. We have worked with the numbers from the past three years and think that we have come up with a way for you to afford it. If you're interested, we would like to take you through the financials and show you how we see this happening."

"If you have a plan that has me owning this place, I'd love to hear it."

Andrew took her through the financials so she would have an idea of the revenue potential as well as the maintenance figures. "We didn't know what you had for a down payment, but we developed several scenarios depending on what you

Making A Difference

could come up with." He then discussed their price and put the whole picture together for her.

Kaliesha nodded, "OK, I see what you're saying. The more I can come up with as a down payment, the lower my mortgage payments will be. I need to see what I could get for my home and how much my investments are worth. Give me a few days and I'll have that information so we can sit down again and go over the details more accurately." She stood, "Thank you for considering me. You've given me a lot to think about and I do my best thinking while I work so now, I need to go finish the laundry."

As she left, the phone rang. Andrew answered, and after responding to some questions, he hung up. Looking at Gregory, "That was Carson Drummond, a journalist who wants to discuss a proposal with us. He's coming over tonight at seven o'clock."

"Did he give you any idea what he wanted to discuss?" Gregory queried.

"He wants to document our role in helping New Brunswick to make same gender marriage legal."

*****

Carson was prompt and showed up at seven. He was an average-looking man in his late twenties who wore round, Harry-Potter style glasses, and had thick, wavey, auburn hair, which was longer on the top. They went out onto the back deck and sat around the table which had been set with refreshments in preparation for the meeting.

Andrew started the conversation, "So, Carson, we're intrigued to hear about who you are, your background, and your proposal on documenting same gender marriage."

Carson thought a minute and started, "I was born and grew up in Saint John and received my Bachelor of Arts degree in journalism from the University of New Brunswick. I grew up on the east side but now live just a few streets over from here. I've worked for the past several years for online publications and I have had articles published which have been well received. I am proud to say I wo a journalism award for my coverage of the pandemic and how it has changed people's lives. I've written two documentary books and my publisher offered me this project. We are coming up on the twentieth anniversary of same gender marriage becoming legal in 2005 both in New Brunswick in June, and in Canada in July. The project is to document the road to that milestone and when I started my research, you and one other couple, Robert Thibodeau and his husband, Victor Rawlings, received a lot of press for your efforts. I've contacted them, and they are willing to be part of this project. They mentioned two other couples who were part of your lawsuit against the province, so I'll be contacting them as well. What else would you like to know?"

Gregory sat up in his chair and leaned forward, "You have your facts straight so that's a good start. If we agree to being part of this project, can we have a chance to read what you're going to submit?"

"I have no problem having you read through any of what I write, but in the end, the editor has the power to overrule anything that I've written. Having said that, my editor is a very fair person and I've not had any issues with her changing the intent of my articles in the past. If anything, her suggestions improve what I write."

Andrew nodded, "I like that approach because we have been misquoted in the past so we would like to make sure what you write is as accurate as possible. If you agree to work with us in a collaborative way, I believe we can agree to go ahead with your project. Do you agree Gregory?"

"I do. I'm wondering, though, how you'll go about documenting everything."

"In the coming weeks I'll be completing a timeline on how same gender rights progressed. Once I have that, I'll plug in the governmental, political, or social issues that came to the forefront along that timeline. This will be factual research to give me a sense of the mood at the time and I'll be using the stories you and the others share to flesh out that timeline. This story will be about you two and follow your perspectives about what was happening during the late 1990s up to the ruling that made same gender marriage legal in 2005. I have enough done on the timeline to start interviews. I'll be contacting the others to add to your story."

Andrew looked agitated, "Whoa! This isn't our story, and we'll not have any part in it if you're making it appear that it was us who did this on our own. So many people contributed to making this happen, and I want their contribution captured. We did not do this on our own."

Carson's face went pale. "Would you agree if we made it a joint story with you two and Robert and Victor while mentioning others' contributions as they happened?"

Andrew calmed and looked to Gregory, "How do you feel about this being a joint story?"

"I agree this isn't just about us so anything that would suggest that would not work for me." He looked at Carson, "If I'm hearing you correctly, I would agree

Making A Difference

if Robert and Victor's contribution was represented as equal to our contribution. We four seemed to be the only gay people in Saint John that would talk with the press at the time. Because we were vocal, they contacted either couple for any story about what was in the news on that day and at the time it was in the news almost daily. Sometimes they would feature all four of us. The reporters would joke about how small the pool of gay people was who would put themselves forward for a story."

"I could use that in the book, don't let me forget that. So, I'm willing to be flexible and I'll look to you for guidance around how the facts roll out but, in the end, I am the author. Are you ok with that?"

Gregory was nodding and Andrew picked up on it before responding, "Carson, I'm getting a collaborative vibe from you so yes, I think we can work together."

"Great! I'll call you by the end of next week and set up four or five interview sessions. I have a six-month schedule to get the rough manuscript together, so we'll be spending a lot of time together in the coming months."

Gregory looked at Carson, "I hope you don't mind me asking but are you gay?"

"No, but my father is and, over the years we have had many conversations about what the mood of society was like, and he mentions both of you by name. It's because of your activism that our family has achieved a sense of freedom. I look forward to our time together."

Making A Difference

Chapter 3

Mackenzie reviewed several documents and reached for her phone. Brock picked up on the third ring, "Hey Bro, I've been trying you all day. I left messages but you haven't returned my calls, what's up?"

"I'm sorry Sis; we've had a minor crisis here at Pine Valley and I've been working all day to resolve it. I did get your messages, but this is the first free time I've had all day. You said there were things we needed to discuss about the foundation, can we do it now?"

"I'd much rather discuss this face to face. Do you think you could spare half an hour sometime soon, like today?"

"I just got in and I'm in bad need of a shower. Can you come here in an hour?"

"Alright, I'll be there." She ended the call and started to make a list of all the things she needed to discuss with him about the foundation.

The idea to set up the foundation came shortly after Brock inherited his fortune from Mammie, their elderly neighbour who passed away eight years before. Brock was the sole heir and he inherited almost 98 million dollars which he has kept secret from everyone but Mackenzie, Andrew, and Gregory. He used some of the money to build the Alice DesRoches Homeless Shelter which Mackenzie now manages. One of her programs provides scholarships to the residents and they get their tuition, books, and accommodation paid. They have had great success and of the ten people who received the bursary, nine completed their post secondary education and found good jobs. Four now work for Brock in different capacities at his garden centre, Pine Valley. At quarter to the hour, she gathered her things together and left to meet Brock.

Brock saw Mackenzie's car enter his driveway and went to the door to greet her. He wrapped his arms around her in a tight hug. "How's my favourite sister?"

Mackenzie relished his hugs, but the favourite sister was an old line that went back to elementary school, but he still got a kick out of it. "Your only sister is doing quite well. The homeless shelter is keeping me busy, and we've been running at 97% occupancy. It kills me to have to turn people away so we might want to talk about an expansion."

"Is that what we need to talk about?"

Making A Difference

"That's not at the top of the list but if we have time, I'd love to start the conversation."

"Come in and we can talk at the dining room table. I know you have a list like you always do, so tell me where we need to start."

"You know me so well!" She put her list on the table in front of her. "We helped twenty-four people last year including the bursaries to the residents of the shelter and this year seems to be ramping up to be a busy one as well. Tonight, I want us to review the five people who we'll chose to help. I know this is a formality as you have allowed me to make many selections on my own, but we're in this together and I want you to know what's happening." She reviewed each of the people, spelling out their circumstances, the financial need, and how much they would grant the person. She then filled him in on how things were going at the shelter and her decision to hire a therapist.

"Hiring a therapist will take a load off of you. I've been asking you to do that for two years, why have you decided to finally do it?"

"Well, I had to admit to myself that I cannot be all things to everyone so I'm stepping down from my Superwoman soapbox and allowing someone to help me. I have the ad developed and I'll be circulating it over the next week. Hopefully I'll have someone hired and in place within the month."

"Good for you Mackenzie. That step off of your soapbox must have been a lulu, but I'm glad you made it. If you need help hiring, I've had lots of experience."

"Thank you. I think I'll wait until I see how many people apply. I'll let you know if I need you."

"Is it time to have the expansion conversation?"

"Since you brought it up, we can. As you know, we're not doling out anywhere near the interest you make on your investments, and I don't see us doing that in the foreseeable future. With that in mind, we could investigate building the extra floor. You looked after putting the necessary structural components in the initial construction to allow for expansion if we needed. I think we need it."

"I've been following the reports you supply me with, and I agree."

"That was fast! When can we start?"

"Whoa. We have a lot of planning to do to see if it's feasible. One thing is, can the residents live there during construction and if not, what do we do with them? I'd like to talk to Andrew and Gregory about this and if it's feasible, I'd hire them to manage the project like they did with the original build. I know they'll bring Dad back as general contractor. I'll call them in the morning but there are things they'll need to check out. Give me a week and I'll see what I can find out."

Making A Difference

*****

Before leaving for Pine Valley, Brock called Andrew. He explained the need to add another floor above the existing residents' floor to house an additional ten residents. They talked about the ease of doing the expansion all because Brock had insisted that the original design incorporate the structural infrastructure for the addition. When Brock asked if they would act as project managers again, Andrew conferred with Gregory, and he came back with a quick yes. They talked about the steps, and Andrew was cautious asking, "Since Anson Wilder designed the shelter and included the structural components for any future expansion, what do you think of hiring him again?"

"I hear concern in your voice, and it's probably about Matthew and Anson having joined forces to open their own architect firm. Don't be concerned. Anson is the right person to do the drawings, but I will not be visiting the firm. This expansion is straight forward so I don't need to be there. I expect the design to be similar, if not identical, to the existing floor so you guys can run with it. Of course, if you need me for anything, let me know."

"We'll contact Anson, and we want your dad to be the general contractor again. We were very pleased with his expertise and eye for quality work, so I'll contact him as well. He's very familiar with every aspect of that building so I don't think he would need the drawings to hire his trades. We'll need them for the necessary permits from the city, but it shouldn't stop us from planning."

"Great, let me know what you find out. One question I'd like you to ask Dad is about whether the expansion can be done with minimal disruption to the running of the shelter. I'm hoping the residents can remain there. I don't have all the knowledge Dad has but, as I see it, the addition could be done without breaking into the existing shelter until the end."

*****

Andrew contacted Anson and discussed the proposed expansion. Anson did not have a copy of the blueprints since all the previous work was done at MacDonald Broadview Architects so he asked if Andrew had a copy of the drawings because he would need them to do the expansion.

Andrew offered, "I do. If you're available right now, I can be there in minutes with an original set."

Making A Difference

"I am, come on over."

Anson didn't see Matthew standing at his door, "Did you hear that conversation?"

"Yes, it was about expansion on Mammie's shelter. Who is coming?"

"Andrew should be here shortly. He's bringing a copy of the blueprints."

They heard the front door and Anson leapt out of his seat to greet Andrew and Gregory. Andrew gave Anson the drawings and he invited them into his office.

Matthew was standing off to the side when Gregory saw him, "Hello Matthew, we haven't seen you in a long time."

"I've been busy and didn't know if I'd run into Brock if I visited '*the manor*', so I've kept to myself."

Andrew broke in, "Matthew, you're always welcome in our home. We love you and Brock, and I'm sure if you met at our place, you both would do fine."

"Thanks, that makes me feel less stressed. I've been concerned since I returned from Dalhousie University."

"We heard that you and Anson joined together to open this firm but didn't know if you were a couple. Either way, we brought your firm some work. We have been hired to investigate the feasibility of doing an expansion to the homeless shelter and be the project managers again if it was a go."

Anson watched the interchange and when he felt it was appropriate, he jumped in. "I have about an hour before our next client arrives and I feel we can do everything we need to do to help you decide. If I remember correctly, the design that was built was created for the sole purpose of a future expansion. The expansion would be to double the number of residential units so the shelter could house 20 residents. Let's look at the drawings and I'll point out what we did and talk about what may be needed that may not be in place."

As Anson began to unroll the drawings, Andrew added, "I believe you looked after all of the key infrastructure points an expansion would require. Can you confirm that?"

Anson studied the drawings and after a few minutes he started pointing out the areas that would be important for the expansion. As he went from one point to the next, he explained what was needed and shook his head each time saying they were in place. "If the building was built to these specifications, the structural components are already in place. If the electrical and plumbing contractors followed what's outlined here, the extending of those systems would be down to simply connecting the addition's wiring and plumbing to the hubs designed for an expansion. The city approved all of the work so unless they skipped over something I'd say we're ready."

"I can get Grant Matheson to verify all of this to make sure. Do you feel comfortable designing the expansion?"

"I don't see any reason why I couldn't. I could have the drawing in a week. I'll duplicate the design from the second floor and make sure everything will fit together."

"You're hired. Let me know when you have the drawings done."

They shook hands to seal the deal.

Andrew and Gregory left the building and Andrew dialed Grant. He explained the idea of the expansion and the result of the meeting with Anson. When he asked Grant if he would be the General Contractor, he told them he would be, he just needed to rearrange some things. He didn't think there would be any issues. They then talked timelines and since the additional level would duplicate the second floor, Grant had what he needed to start preliminary conversations with the trades. Before ending the call, they agreed to reconnect by mid next week with a status of where they were.

Chapter 4

Brock let himself into *'the manor'* with his key and crept into the kitchen. He found Kaleisha, back to him, busying herself with the spice drawer. He tiptoed over to her and wrapped his arms around her. She screamed, turned around with a red face and slapped his shoulder, "Brock, you're bad!"

Brock laughed and gave her a proper hug. "It seems like forever since we've seen each other; how are you and Roger doing? Are you still as in love as ever?"

"Roger is such a wonderful guy! We haven't gotten bored with each other yet and some days we act like love-struck teenagers. Life couldn't be better unless….."

"Don't stop and leave me guessing!"

"Oh, alright. Did you hear that the guys have offered for me to buy *'the manor'*?"

Brock's surprise was evident, "No, I saw them last week, but we had other things to talk about and my schedule hasn't allowed me much time to socialize. When did this happen? Tell me everything."

She knew the guys were close to Brock and had assumed they would have mentioned their proposal to him. She started telling him all the details they had discussed and what she had done to determine her down payment. "I think I'll be able to do it, I'm just waiting on a couple of investments and then I'll have all of my information."

"So, they will hold the mortgage. What a bonus! I think they really want you to own this because they'll know the reputation of Mahogany Manor will be guaranteed. That would be so important to them. When do you think you'll take ownership?"

Kaleisha did a double take and looked at Brock, "Taking ownership is shocking to me. Of course, I know I'll be the owner but having you ask that question makes it too real. Am I ready? Anyway, when I have the information on my investments I'll meet with the guys and determine if I can do it. They have promised they'll do whatever I need them to do to make this happen."

"I have no doubt they want you to have it. I'm so happy for you! If something happens where you don't have enough money, come and see me; I can help. Mammie left me a bit of money and Pine Valley Garden Centre is doing so

Making A Difference

well, so whatever the guys can't help with, I'm sure I can help with whatever money you need."

"Thank you, Brock!" She gave him another hug, "I hope I won't need it, but your offer provides me with so much comfort! How long ago did you stop your grounds keeping role here?"

"I left just before I started working on the garden centre so that would be after my Botany degree, so the summer of 2019. I hired Paul to replace me before I left; how's he making out?"

"He's doing well but he isn't you. You seemed to have a special relationship with the garden. To Paul it's just a job. I don't feel the same sense of commitment. Of course, you were full time working inside and out and Paul is only working the gardens. You had everything in such good shape, he only has to maintain. I notice that the guys spend some time out there every week when Paul isn't here. They never did that while you worked here."

Brock blushed, "Stop, you're embarrassing me."

Kaleisha laughed and she teased him even more.

"Ok, I'm going to leave if you don't stop."

"Alright, I'll stop. What's new with you?"

Brock thought about his answer, "My business is going well, Mom and Dad are busy, Mackenzie is making Mammie's homeless shelter her own and I'm hiring some of the residents for the Garden Centre."

Kaleisha knew she was about to ask a sensitive question, but she needed to know, "Do you ever see Matthew around?"

To hear Matthew's name used to be hard for him but it had become easier over the years. When Matthew suggested they separate before he went to Halifax to finish his architect education, it was difficult for Brock to hear. He believed if someone didn't want to be in a relationship, they couldn't be forced. He still loved Matthew who he seemed to move on a lot easier than Brock. Matthew has had several boyfriends he had heard about, but none of the relationships lasted more than a year. He decided Kalesha deserved an answer, "Usually from a distance until a couple of days ago when he dropped into Pine Valley. When he entered, he made a beeline to me, and we talked for a few minutes. He said he was there to look at some shrubs for his place, but he never went near them, at least that I know. It was a busy day, and I was being pulled in several directions so I couldn't spend time with him. When I was free to talk, he was gone."

"You still love him, don't you?"

Making A Difference

"I do and I think I always will. I had to face the fact he just doesn't want me. It makes me sad, but I need to let go of the notion he will come back so I can move on. When it first happened four years ago, I thought he'd get his need not to be together out of his system and come back. As the years went by it became apparent, he wasn't coming back. At first, I poured myself into my studies and the building of Pine Valley but as things settled, I realized I was avoiding reality. I talked it over with Dad and he suggested counselling, so I've been doing that for just over a year now. I find it's a lot to deal with but I'm hoping it'll get easier with time."

"Have you dated anyone?"

"I didn't for the first two years because I expected that when he came home after he graduated as an architect, we would reconnect. When that didn't happen, it hit me hard and I signed on to a dating site and tried a few guys, but they were not Matthew. I think I understand what a rebound relationship is and why it's bad. I found myself comparing and it just wasn't fair to any of the guys. I realized I needed to get my shit together first. Therapy is helping some."

Kaleisha decided to change topics to give Brock a break. "Have the guys told you about a journalist interviewing them because of their activism and how they helped make same-gender marriage legal in New Brunswick?"

"I haven't really connected with them for a few weeks. When did this start?"

She explained what she knew, the initial phone call, the subsequent meeting, and then the interviews that were happening two or three times a week. She told Brock about discussing the project with the guys and what she learned about other activism they participated in prior to getting involved with the fight for marriage equality.

Brock added to the story, "I know they took the federal government, the municipal government, and the Provincial Government to task for various discriminations and they even placed a Human Rights complaint against the Member of Parliament when she refused to meet with them but opened her doors to the Christian community. They felt they were being discriminated against because they're gay. They also told me they took their employer to task to have equality in their employee benefits."

"I heard some of those things, but I didn't know it all. They really did a lot to advance gay rights."

"They did and I'm glad this journalist is writing a book on their struggle; it's about time they were recognized for their contribution. I think they should get some award."

"Are there awards they could receive?"

Making A Difference

Brock looked pensive and, after a minute, responded, "I really don't know, but I guess I could find out."

*****

"Good morning, Kaleisha! You look quite happy today; could it be anything to do with the information you needed?" Andrew asked as she entered with a bigger than usual smile.

"I have my numbers from my investments and what I could get for my house. We need to sit down and work out what this deal will look like."

"We're leaving shortly for a couple of meetings we need to attend but we expect to be back by mid afternoon. If you can have your work done, we could sit down and see what this will look like."

She clapped her hands in child-like enthusiasm. "I'll be ready when you are. I'm looking forward to understanding the details."

Gregory broke in, "Some of the guests have eaten early so you have six more who should be down within fifteen minutes. I've set up the fruit plates and they are in the fridge. The batter for the pancakes is in the bowl by the stove. We have three rooms to tidy and two to turn over so today is a lighter day than usual. We'll see you when we return."

As they left, the house came to life when all six remaining guests came down the staircase in short order. Kaleisha welcomed them, "Good morning, everyone! Take a seat and I'll start serving your breakfast."

Kaleisha chatted as she served everyone, using her talents to make each guest feel special. She answered questions, gave out any requested information, and noted who had left and who was just going up to their rooms. She worked in the kitchen and was finished when she heard the last guest leave. She wasted no time tidying the three rooms which needed it and she moved into the two rooms needing to be cleaned for new guests in the afternoon. By the time the guys returned, she had everything in order and had checked one of the couples in when they arrived early. She was working at the check-in desk when they came through the door.

Andrew continued into the kitchen with a parcel and returned to the check-in desk and joined into the conversation Gregory and Kaleisha were having, "The last couple is coming after supper, so we have time right now to go to our private quarters and put all of the information together. Now, you get to see what this looks like for you."

Kaleisha pounced, "Then what are we waiting for? Let's go!"

Making A Difference

They arranged the information on the table and took the numbers Kaleisha gave them. Andrew explained, "If you can sell your home for that price and you have that amount in investments, you have a sizeable down payment. Let's use those numbers and see what your mortgage will be." After several clicks on his laptop Andrew turned the screen around and showed Kaleisha the spreadsheet he had explained a few weeks ago when they first met to discuss the opportunity. "What do you think?"

"Given the numbers you discussed with me about the revenue and the cost to maintain the business, I feel I can do this unless I'm missing something. What do you both think?"

Gregory was the first to reply, "I've been running all kinds of numbers since we had our first chat, and this is one of the best scenarios. What do you think Andrew?"

"Looking at these figures tells me you can afford *'the manor'*! Kaleisha, if you want to say yes, I believe you have bought yourself a business!"

"YES!!! How do we make this legal?"

"We'll contact our lawyer and draw up the necessary agreements and send them to your lawyer. They'll take it from there."

"When can we do this?"

"First you need to sell your home and convert your investments into cash. Once that's done, we can finalize the sale and *'the manor'* is yours!"

Making A Difference

Chapter 5

Martha and Grant arranged the chairs for the Pflag meeting. They had taken over running the meetings when Andrew and Gregory stepped down about two years ago. With both of their kids out of the house and done with their university degrees they decided to give back to the community. They credited Pflag with bringing their family back together after it was torn apart when they kicked Brock out of their lives when he came out to them. It took many months of going to Pflag meetings, each seeing a therapist, lots of reading, and constant hounding from Mackenzie to get them to see Brock's being gay as not a terrible shame. Only then did the Matheson family come together to begin rebuilding their relationships.

When Andrew approached them about taking over, they both had doubts they could help anyone. He pointed out how well the people attending the meetings responded to them when they told their story. Only after a guarantee from Andrew that he would support them if they needed him, did they agree to take the meetings over. In the two years since, both Martha and Grant had grown in their confidence and only had to call on Andrew for assistance one time.

As the room filled, Martha remembered her first meeting. She had been petrified to speak, and she gave her name during the introductions and left the meeting two hours later without having said anything more. She wondered what Grant was thinking. She remembered how adamant he was that he wouldn't go to a meeting because he felt like it was a cult and Martha was being brainwashed. It wasn't until she threatened to end their marriage that he agreed to attend. After that first time, he blossomed and didn't miss a meeting after that.

Grant started the meeting and Martha took her turn by starting the introductions. She recognized herself in some of the new attendees and hoped they would stick it out. She was amazed at the new terms that had come to the forefront and how some people used them with such ease. She found she had to do research to get comfortable with the pronouns some people identified with and the new terminology like cis gender, non-binary, asexual, etc. which seemed were being introduced every month. She leaned on Pflag Canada to help her understand the newest terms knowing new ones were right around the corner. As she thought back to how ignorant she was about the different aspect of human sexuality, she had to admit this certainly was an education.

Making A Difference

Grant looked at his watch, "We have about ten minutes left. Is there anything that hasn't been said that needs to be said."

The room was quiet and just as Grant was about to close the meeting, one of the new attendees raised his hand. Grant realized he hadn't given his name, so he acknowledged him. "Do you have something you need to say?"

"I passed during introductions, but my name is Liam. I need to say thank you to everyone being so open and sharing their information. Over the past months I've been bullied on my way to school, during breaks between classes, and after school on my way home. It's always the same three guys, and I can't seem to get away from them. I was ready to give up and I looked into ways to kill myself." Tears started to flow down his cheeks, but he continued, "I seem to be alone. My so-called friends deserted me when the bullies attacked me and never came back. No one at school seemed to care and I was ready to end it, but I read about tonight's meeting. This meeting gave me the spark of hope to reach out hoping I'd find someone, anyone who would care." He sobbed and Chloe, the girl sitting next to him, leaned over, gave him a hug and held him until the sobbing subsided.

The silence in the room was palpable.

Chloe released the hug and looked Liam in the eye, "I've seen you around Queen Elizabeth High School and I go there. I want to be your friend and be with you during those times when the bullies attack. You know, strength in numbers."

Martin, a boy about Liam's age spoke up, "Me too. We have a Gay Straight Alliance at school, and I was always afraid to join but the three of us could join together. It would be great to find more people like us or others who'd be allies."

Liam wiped his eyes and smiled, "You would do this for me? I don't know what to say."

Chloe hooked her arm in his and responded, "Say you'll be our friend!"

"I want you both as my friends."

Martin spoke up, "After the meeting, let's share our contact information and spend some time together over the weekend getting to know each other. This meeting will be the secret that binds us together."

"It's a deal!" Liam's smile made his face light up.

Martha spoke, "I love these meetings! Our time is up but if anyone else needs to speak, I'll stay to listen." No one spoke. "Ok, remember our next meeting is the third Friday of the month at 7:00.

As they collected their information to leave, the door opened and one of the women from the meeting stepped in.

"Did you forget something?" Grant asked.

Making A Difference

"Yes, I forgot to introduce myself. I'm Molly Fraser and this was my first meeting. I listened as you explained a bit of your story and it resonated with me. My husband, Jim, and I kicked Callie, our daughter, out of our house for being a lesbian. One afternoon I went home from work not feeling well and I heard a noise coming from Callie's room. I opened the door to find her and another girl making out in the bed. I blew up and kicked the other girl out and called Jim to come home early. We had a heated confrontation and told her to get out. She left and we don't know where she went. It's been three weeks and I've been worried sick, but Jim believes she'll come to her senses and come home. I don't think so. Callie is quite stubborn. I've checked with her friends, but they haven't been helpful. Callie would have told them not to give us any information. I've even tried the shelters in the area, but she hasn't checked in there. I even called the police but since she's eighteen and we kicked her out, she can't be considered a missing person, but I want to find her. I need help."

Martha's heart melted hearing a story so like her own. "Molly, why don't you come back to our home for a cup of tea, and we can start to help get you on the road to getting your family back together."

Molly let a held breath out, "I'd welcome that but are you sure it isn't too late?"

"Not at all. Here's our address, do you know where it is?"

"I'm not familiar with the uptown area. I've heard of the street, but I don't think I could find it easily."

"Well, you can follow us there. We're ready and the commissionaire is waiting to lock the door so let's go."

Molly followed Martha and Grant and parked behind them in their driveway. "Is it OK to park here?"

Grant assured her it was OK, and they went into the house together. Martha got the water boiling and Grant showed her to a seat at the kitchen table.

Martha put some banana bread on a plate and placed it on the table with cups of tea for Molly and herself while Grant got a beer from the fridge.

Martha gave Molly a lot more detail about the blow up that removed Brock from their lives and began to explain how they started to put things back together.

Grant explained how homophobic he was but omitted telling Molly about the abuse by Father Mike. He talked about his feelings and how Anne, his therapist, helped him face many old and incorrect beliefs. He went to the living room and returned with several books and in general terms, explained how they helped him. He also offered to speak with Jim if she thought it would help.

Making A Difference

Molly listened and asked questions here and there throughout their conversation. She seemed at peace, and they thought she found comfort in what they had explained about their situation.

Martha picked through the books on the table and handed one to Molly, "I think this book opened my eyes to a different world. I suggest you start reading it with Jim so you can have some good discussion. If he doesn't want to read it, you read it and you can use me to discuss the things you need to clarify. I did this with Mackenzie, our daughter, and we both found it to be a great resource. Mackenzie knew so much more than I did, and she learned things. What do you think?"

"I'll read it. I don't think Jim will, but I won't know until I try."

At the door, she gave both Grant and Martha hugs and when she released, "Thank you both for being so kind. I was at my wits end and had no one to turn to. I saw the ad for tonight's meeting and decided I needed to start somewhere. Even though I didn't say anything at the meeting, you both made me feel I could approach you. After the meeting I sat in my car wrestling with whether I should go back in. I'm glad I did. I have your numbers to keep in touch and you have my cell number. I promise I'll read this book. Thank you again, bye."

Martha and Grant watched in silence as Molly got in her car and backed out onto the road. They looked to each other, and Martha said, "This is why we're in Pflag. To give back. I know we're making a difference in people's lives, and it feels so rewarding!" She could see Grant was mulling something over in his mind, so she let him have the time he needed.

Grant opened up, "I know how embarrassed I'm about how I handled things. I hope Jim isn't as pigheaded as I was."

Martha laughed, "Is that even possible? You had to have been the master of pigheadedness at the time." She gave a gentle punch on his arm and added, "Just kidding!"

He spun her around and nuzzled her neck. She laid her head back and revelled in the sensations he was causing. Grabbing her hand, he started leading her toward the stairs until she paused, "Don't you think we should lock the house up and turn out the lights first?"

"That can wait. We have more important things to do."

She thought for a few seconds, "Ohhhhhh! You're so right, it can wait. Beat you up the stairs!"

"Not if I can help it!" He leapt three steps up and ran the rest of the way with Martha chasing after.

Making A Difference

Chapter 6

Anson was working on the drawing for the shelter and asked Matthew to join him so he could discuss some thinking about the design. Mathew listened and gave a few ideas they flushed out before they were both content. "There, now I just need to finish the drawing and I can call Andrew. I'm so glad they chose me again. I thought if it was ever going to happen, they would have remained with MacDonald Broadview Architects."

"Where you were the original architect, I can see why they came back to you. The more we get our name out there, the more work we'll get."

"Our vision for Erb & Wilder Architects to be the '*sought-after*' architectural firm in the city is a few years out, but I'm confident it will happen. We started out slow but in the two years we have been together, the firm has grown from just the two of us to us and a receptionist." He gave a little chuckle.

Matthew chuckled along with him, "Yes, we're heading for the big time! On another topic, how was the theatre last night?"

"I felt it was good, but Charles was thrilled with the show. We see so many things the same but every so often, we can see things so differently. I guess that's what keeps our relationship fresh. Do you know we'e been together eight years?"

"Yes, I guess it has been eight years. Brock and I've been apart four years." Matthew added and trailed off into deep thought.

Anson noticed his mood, "What's going on with you Matthew? It's almost as if you are regretting your decision."

"I went to speak with Brock last week and he only spent a few minutes before he had to go somewhere to deal with an issue. He was all business, and I didn't feel any warmth."

"What do you expect? You told him you didn't want to be a couple before you headed off to Halifax. He never saw that coming and it hit him hard. Charles and I had him over to our place often when it first happened, but he was mourning your leaving and always went home early. Once he accepted you weren't coming back to tell him you made a mistake, he put all of his energy into his MBA degree and started building his garden centre using your drawings."

"Yes, I was pleased he used them. They came out of a project I did for one of my courses. I used the Dunes from Prince Edward Island as my inspiration and brought in the things Brock used to talk about when he would dream out loud. I got an A+ and gave the plans to Brock as a gift. I didn't know he had built it until I returned home. Mom had told me, and I drove by it one day. I almost went in but felt I shouldn't since I had Anthony with me."

"I didn't get to know Anthony very well. He only lasted a couple of months. Then there was Christopher, then Joseph, and finally Collin. He lasted an entire year, what broke you up?"

Matthew looked off into space, "Collin was a dream who became a nightmare. I suspected he was cheating and one day I went home and found him in bed with my ex, Christopher. I threw them both out and I've been single for the past two months. There's a big part of me regrets leaving Brock."

"You've never discussed this before. Why, exactly, did you leave Brock?"

"You know, when I review the past four years, I think I wanted to experience more of the gay life that's written about online and in magazines. It all sounds so exciting and cosmopolitan. I guess I convinced myself that it was more exciting than it was for me. I searched, but never found it. I must have dated, and I'm counting the one-night stands, about forty guys over the two years I was in Halifax. There was a part of me that bought into the lust and excitement, but I've since learned the casual lifestyle isn't for me. What I know is, I really crave the stability I had with Brock, but I didn't realize it until I failed at every relationship I've had since." Matthew, used to being the clown, was being genuine.

Anson watched as Matthew went solemn, "I've never seen you like this. You're always happy-go-lucky, and nothing seems to bother you. Have you thought about talking to a therapist?"

"Mom suggested that as well. Maybe I need to see one. Do you know of any you'd recommend?"

"Several friends are finding Richard Paris to be quite helpful. They even gave me his business card." He dug through his desk, pulled out a card, and passed it to Matthew.

*****

Gregory waited until Andrew finished the call and asked, "From what I could glean from your conversation, Anson must have our drawing ready."

"Yes, he can meet us in half an hour so we should change out of our pajama pants and into street-worthy attire."

They said good-bye to Kaleisha and walked down to Canterbury Street. Anson happened to be out in the front talking with Sheila, the receptionist, so he

Making A Difference

greeted them when they arrived. He took Andrew and Gregory into his office and had the drawings laid out on his table. They reviewed the drawings as Anson took them through how the structure was expanded on the existing infrastructure. "There was a bit of tweaking but because of the work that was done with the original build, it was easy to design. One area we had to alter most was the staircase." He showed the issue that he had found and then explained his solution.

Andrew scanned the drawing one more time, "It looks like you've done it again, Anson. When can I have eight copies to give to the general contractor?"

"If you have fifteen minutes, I'll get Shelia to run them off." He left for a few minutes and when he returned, he started casual conversation. "So, what's new at *'the manor'*?"

The guys explained that they were selling it to Kaleisha, and they were just waiting on the sale of her home. She was accepting offers until tomorrow and has a few that look very promising so soon it will be a done deal."

"Where will you live?"

Gregory lit up, "You and Charles have been with Brock to our cottage on the Kingston Peninsula. We bought that several years ago when we decided we would sell *'the manor'* when we retired. We're having work done to make it a year-round home so it should be complete in another week or so for us to move in after that."

"That'll be a big change for you. Won't you miss the uptown area?"

"We're both country boys and the cottage gives us that closeness to nature we have been missing living in the city. We have clocked the distance and time and we'll be able to commute quite easily anytime we want to come to the city for visiting friends, restaurants, entertainment, and shopping. For now, we think it will work out quite well."

Matthew came around the corner, "I couldn't help but hear that you're selling *'the manor'*?" I didn't get all the details, but I wanted to congratulate you. How many years have you had it?"

Andrew leaned forward, "It was thirty years last month. We're getting older, and it's time for us to enjoy other pursuits. We had talked about travelling but the pandemic put those plans on hold. Now that things have straightened out and most of the world is vaccinated, we feel our chance to travel is now."

Matthew high-fived both Andrew and Gregory, "Good for you! Kaleisha will do a great job and maintain the reputation Mahogany Manor Bed and Breakfast has attained under your ownership."

Making A Difference

Sheila walked around the corner and stood quietly while the last part of the conversation ended. Anson saw her and motioned her to come forward. "Here are eight copies, but if you need more, let me know." Once she handed them to Andrew and Gregory, she returned to her desk.

Andrew looked to Anson, "Do you have the bill ready?"

"I should have printed that off, but I wanted to make sure you were happy with the drawings first and forgot when we got into conversation." He sat down and pressed a few keys. "I just printed it on Sheila's printer. We can get it on the way out."

Sheila had it folded in an envelope. Anson took it out and reviewed it with the guys. They wrote a cheque, and handed it to Anson, "Thank you for your great work and quick turn-around. We'll recommend Erb and Wilder Architects to all of our friends!"

"Thank you, we appreciate you coming to us!"

As they walked home, Andrew called Grant and told him he had the drawings, and they would be home in ten minutes. Grant told him he would be over to pick them up. They arrived home just as Grant was pulling into the yard. They met him at the truck and invited him in to review the drawings together.

Gregory unrolled one set on the table and the three gathered around. Andrew pointed out the things Anson had pointed out to him and explained the stairway change.

Grant nodded after each area was identified and gave his approval. He took several sets and announced, "I have the trades lined up and will get the permits for everything in one visit to City Hall. I'm hoping we can start the addition in under a month."

Gregory needed to ask, "Will the residents have to move out?"

Grant thought for several long seconds, "I don't see any reason to have them move out as long as we look after their safety. We'll build a protective tunnel from the street to allow people to go inside and we'll do the same to all fire exits. We need the people to be able to enter and exit without concerns of falling construction equipment and materials. I don't expect we'll disturb the second floor until we run the electrical and plumbing from the hubs that were set up, and the final disturbance will be when we cut out for the staircase. The only inconvenience would be the construction noise throughout the day."

Andrew nodded, "I think Mackenzie will manage that better than having to find alternate accommodations for the residents during construction. Keep us informed about the permits and when you need any money."

Making A Difference

"Will do. I'm looking forward to working with you again. Now, I'm off to City Hall!"

Chapter 7

Brock was moving some trees around in the side yard to make sure all the trees had a fair chance of being chosen. When he was using a dolly while backing up to put the tree in the right place, he hit something, lost his footing, and stumbled backward. He didn't hit the ground like he expected but the fall was aborted by a set of strong arms clad in plaid flannel. When he looked up, a handsome face with a black stubble smiled down on him, "Thanks for catching me. I'm lucky you were right there, that could have been a nasty fall."

The rugged face smiled, "My pleasure. I've been enjoying watching you work so when you mis-stepped into that potted tree, I saw what was about to happen and rushed in to catch you. By the way, my name is Dirk Harrison." He put his hand out.

Brock took Dirk's hand, "Glad to meet you. I'm Brock Matheson."

"So, you work here. I was hoping to find the right tree for my front yard. The old fella that has lived in the front right corner died, and I had to have it removed. The corner looks so empty, I thought I'd buy a mature tree and set things to right."

After discussing the type of tree he was looking for, Brock showed him several, but none seemed to be the right one for Dirk. As they walked from tree to tree, they chatted. Dirk explained that he was self employed as an IT developer. He had developed and sold a popular app, one which Brock used on his phone. Brock told Dirk he was the owner of Pine Valley Garden Centre.

He then showed Dirk other trees and explained the pros and cons of each. There was something about the oak tree Brock showed him. He kept going back to it after declining tree after tree and after looking at almost all the trees, decided the oak was the one.

"Would you like it delivered?" Brock asked hoping he would say yes. He was attracted to Dirk and wanted to spend more time with him.

"That would be perfect. When would you be able to deliver it?"

"I could take it over later this afternoon. Would you be home?"

Dirk smiled, "Today is my day off and I plan to go right home and stay there. I'll be working in the garden and preparing the hole to plant this majestic beast."

Making A Difference

Brock secured a SOLD marker to the tree and wrote Dirk's name on it. "Come with me" He started walking to the sales area and continued their conversation on the way. "When we take your payment, we'll get your address and phone number." After the sale was done, they talked for a few minutes before Brock was called away. Before leaving he said to Dirk, "I'll call when I'm leaving. See you later."
*****

Dirk lived in an upscale neighbourhood and as Brock approached, he spotted Dirk with his shirt off finishing the hole. He had streaks of mud smeared across his forehead and speckled down his amazing torso. Having spent so much time on Dirk's body, he never noticed his home, an impressive modern structure which told Brock Dirk was doing well for himself.

Brock parked as close to the spot as he dared and lowered the tree on the lift to about three feet from the opening. They took a few minutes to decide the best process to get the tree into position. Because of the weight, they worked together and slid it closer, removed the burlap, and Dirk directed Brock as he slowly backed his way toward the hole. One final lift had the tree in place. They watered it well and shoveled soil around it. Talking easily as they worked, they continued to learn more about each other.

Dirk used a level to make sure the tree was straight and stood back just to make sure. He then filled the hole with water and as it drained down, buried the root ball.

Brock was impressed with Dirk's effectiveness, "If you ever want a job at the garden centre, I have a position for you!"

Dirk winked, "I bet you do." He blushed and couldn't believe he was being so forward, "Sorry for that, my mouth has a mind of its own. Are you going right back?"

"I don't have to rush back. I'd like a drink of water if that's possible." Dirk grabbed the hose and passed it to Brock. The surprise look made Dirk laugh.

"I'm just kidding, come into the house and we can sit and chat."

They walked in the house and, after dusting his clothes off, Brock raised his head to find Dirk had removed his pants and socks and stood in just a pair of black silky boxer briefs. "My clothing was disgusting; I hope you don't mind."

Brock was startled but loving it, "I don't mind at all! Just so you know, you're wearing my favourite brand."

Making A Difference

Dirk smiled, he liked Brock's answer, "The kitchen is right there, and the glasses are on the left. Make yourself at home, I'm going to jump in the shower."

He watched Dirk's muscles work as he walked down the hall. Just before going through the door, he looked back at Brock. Dirk smiled and disappeared. Brock's mind was working overtime and he thought about following. No sooner had he put his fantasy to rest and turned to get water, he felt a presence and then a hand on his.

He turned and Dirk winked, "Tell me if I'm reading you wrong but I think you might enjoy a shower too." He took Brock's hand and led him down the hall.

Brock didn't hesitate.

When they made it into the bedroom, Dirk pressed Brock against the wall with a slow sensuous kiss. Brock responded. It had been such a long time since he had kissed anyone and he felt a bit awkward but soon got over it.

Dirk pulled his head back and looked into Brock's eyes, "I've had my eyes on you for a while but wasn't sure if you liked guys. I've never seen you with anyone."

Brock smiled, "That's a long story that I'll tell you but not until after our shower. I have other things on my mind." He pressed his excitement against Dirk. "See."

Dirk started kissing down his neck as he undid the buttons on Brock's shirt and slid it off his shoulders. He ran his hands over Brock's chest and relished the heat as he took one of Brock's nipples between his lips and tongued it softly sending shivers of delight through Brock's body. Brock threw his head back and moaned. Dirk opened Brock's pants and slid them down his legs to puddle at his feet. Brock kicked them off and got rid of his socks leaving the two standing together in very similar black silky boxer briefs. Dirk pressed himself against Brock and together they moaned at the sensation. They each slid their hands into the other's waistband and in unison set them free. Dirk took Brock's hand and led him into the shower. Brock stood out of the spray while Dirk adjusted the temperature and pulled Brock into the warmth. They embraced, kissed, and explored each others' bodies. They lathered each other and rubbed their bodies together causing each to slide off the other. They laughed but enjoyed the sensations. Brock began kissing down Dirk's body and knelt to take Dirk's cock into his mouth. Dirk savoured the feelings and moaned, "Oohhhh fuuccckkkk!" as he tweaked his own nipples. Making low guttural responses to Brock's ministering, Dirk tensed, started quaking, and released his passion.

Making A Difference

When Dirk quieted, he pulled Brock up to embrace him. He explored and kissed his way down to massage Brock's cock while he continued until he popped one of his testicles into his mouth. Brock was cautious but excited and moaned despite himself. As he responded to Dirk's expert maneuvers, he felt his climax mounting and when Dirk slid a finger into him, he exploded with exuberance and sunk down to the floor. Water streamed over them as the kissed. After composing themselves, they helped each other complete the shower. They dried off and collapsed onto the bed.

Dirk rolled onto his side facing Brock and offered, "I'm ready to hear the story."

Brock told him about meeting Matthew and how they became great friends and then started a deeper relationship. He talked about all the good and how he started noticing something was different. He put it off to the demands of university but one day Matthew suggested they separate while he went to Halifax to complete his degree in architecture. At that point, Dirk saw the effect his story telling had on Brock and suggested he didn't have to continue.

Brock looked him in the eyes and continued, "Thanks but I think I need to talk about this. It's doing me little good keeping it pent up inside hoping for something that isn't going to happen."

"You still love him." Dirk whispered into the sadness that filled the room.

Brock lowered his head, "Yes, I guess I do but it's been four years, so I know it's over. I thought we were friends, but he never contacts me. I have to face it; he has a new life and I have to accept I'm not part of it."

Dirk crooked his index finger and placed it under Brock's chin. He applied a little force and raised his head until they were eye to eye, "I think you're pretty special, and I'd like to see you. How do you feel about that?"

"I like who you are, and I'd like to see you too." Brock smiled and winked.

They hugged and lay there talking about their lives. Brock's stomach growled and Dirk suggested, "I have a kitchen full of food, how about we get up and make some supper?"

Brock agreed and when he went to get dressed, Dirk threw the doors of his closet open and offered, "Here, we're about the same size, and you don't want to put on those sweaty clothes, so choose anything you need. I already know we wear the same underwear and I have some new ones if you'd like them."

They dressed while they chatted and walked together to the kitchen. Dirk opened the fridge and asked, "Do you like vegetables?"

"I like almost everything. What did you have in mind?"

Making A Difference

"I thought a stir-fry would be good."

Brock's phone sounded. "Excuse me, it's the garden centre and I need to take it." It was a short call. "They need the delivery truck, I'm sorry, but I have to go."

Dirk frowned but then brightened, "You take the truck back and I'll have supper ready when you return."

"That would work for me as long as you don't mind."

Dirk smiled, "I want to spend time with you so hurry home."

"You're a gem; how come you have not been snatched up? I'll be here in forty minutes."

Dirk thought of his answer, "You don't have time right now, but I also have a story to tell you when you return."

*****

Brock was back when he said he would be, and the food was ready. Dirk had the table set and he poured glasses of white wine when he heard Brock's car. When Brock walked in, he made a beeline over to Dirk and gave him a kiss.

Dirk smiled and returned the kiss, "I'm liking this already, let's eat."

They had a steady conversation as they ate when there was a pause, Brock asked, "Is this a good time to tell your story? I've been thinking what it would be during my drive here."

"If you're ready, I am too. I haven't told to anyone besides family but there is something about you that makes me feel comfortable." Dirk began a love story that turned into a marriage. "Douglas and I were happy and had great plans for the future." Dirk's eyes watered, he admonished himself, and continued, "One afternoon I received a call. Douglas had passed out at work, and he was sent to the hospital by ambulance. He had an aneurysm and died before I got there." Tears were flowing down his face, and he wiped them away with his sleeve. "I didn't even get to say goodbye. That was almost five years ago."

Brock went over to Dirk and hauled his limp frame up into a hug, "I'm so sorry."

Chapter 8

Brock and Mackenzie arrived at their parents' house to start unpacking the boxes from Father Mike's estate and try to get some order to things. They sat at the dining room table and all four agreed on a plan of attack. As each took a cluster of documents from the box, they made notes to document and maintain the sequence of the information. They felt this was important in case Father Mike had arranged the content in some specific order. It was painstaking work, and it took a while before a pattern began to show. Once they spotted it, they checked to see if all groupings had the same pattern, and they did. This was the first breakthrough of many as they approached suppertime and they called for a break. They ate at the kitchen table and discussed how they were feeling about the work they had done.

Grant summed up his impression, "It looks like Father Mike categorized the documents by each diocese for the initial abuse by the priest and then followed that priest as the church moved him around to either hide the abuse or put him in treatment. Mackenzie, do you remember the work you and Ben were doing for me back in 2016 and you found that movie about how the church hides the abuse?"

As Mackenzie listened to her father's question, her face lit up, "Yes, that movie was called, Spotlight. After watching it with Ben, we saw the similarities to the data we were gathering. It seems the Church was aware of the abuse but hid it from the public and did little to deal with it other than move priests around. The documents Father Mike gathered will probably point to similar behaviours in the higher echelon within the Church. I think the information we have will deal with abuse in Canada, but I could be wrong."

Brock raised a point, "As I was looking through the documents, there were names of some victims, but I can bet there are more. Dad, didn't you say the bishop didn't know about you being abused? Even if there is one victim they didn't know about, that would still amount to a lot of children. I watched Spotlight after Mackenzie told me about it and it makes me believe this issue is far bigger than two boxes. If we were to do anything, we need to understand so much. Like the movie brings out, the abuse was a bigger issue than even they expected."

Martha started wringing her hands and Brock couldn't ignore her anxiety, "Mom, you seem troubled by this conversation; what are you thinking?"

Making A Difference

"The deeper we get into this, the scarier it is for me. Like I said before. I feel badly for the victims."

Grant tried to calm her, "Honey, we have only agreed to go this first step and we may not go farther. Let's get a handle on what we have in those boxes and then we can determine what, if anything, we'll do next."

"OK, but I just can't get beyond this getting as big as I'm thinking it could be. I do know I don't want our family to be front and centre in whatever the next steps are." Martha's face was tight with stress, and it left its mark on the other three.

Brock stepped in, "Mom, we don't yet know where this might lead, so if we promise we won't do anything unless all four of us agree, will that help you?"

"Yes, that will help. I have no problem finishing the step we're working on and if we all have to agree to the next step, I'm game to continue." She looked each one in the eyes for a few seconds before moving to the next, "Now, you have to promise me."

Each one voiced a strong, "I promise."

Martha breathed a sigh of relief, "Thank you. Now, let's get back to work."

They worked for three more hours and decided to call it a day. They agreed to leave everything where it sat and continue the next Sunday.

When Mackenzie and Brock left, he invited her in to talk. They got some tea and sat around the dining table.

"Mom is really stressed, and I really don't know where we're headed but I can't see either you or me letting this drop. It just isn't who we are."

Mackenzie frowned, "But we promised."

Brock winked, "And I intend to keep our promise but it doesn't mean we have to let it drop."

"OK, what's up in that head of yours? You wouldn't be saying that unless you already have a plan so let me in on it."

He smiled, "Remember in the movie Spotlight, who did the investigation?"

"A group of journalists." She brightened, "Are you suggesting we give the information to a journalist and let them run with it?"

"That or some version of that so our involvement is the supplier of the information. We still need to understand what we have so we can sell the idea to them, but we won't have to be personally involved. I think we create a win-win with something being done with the information and we keep the promise we made to Mom. I think she will go along with this."

Mackenzie smiled, "This is brilliant! I think we can get her to agree."

Making A Difference

"We just have to understand what we have first." He switched topics, "Now that we have that out of the way, let's talk about our philanthropy. Have any new opportunities come to light?"

"Nothing for a while, but I've been so busy getting ready to hire the therapist for the shelter. I really have been negligent, sorry."

Brock didn't want her to feel badly, "You have to agree we have been doing some good work with the charity. We're paying for university and community college for the residents at the homeless shelter and I hired five of them for the garden centre. We really have made a difference in their lives, but I want to make sure we don't miss anyone."

Makenzie suggested, "Maybe it's time to advertise. We can still oversee the charity, but advertising will make it known."

Brock thought for a few moments and said, "I've been hesitant to do that, but I think you're right. Can you look into this?"

"Sure, in my spare time. OK, I'm kind of joking but I have the hiring to do and the shelter expansion to plan around but once that slows down, I can put some energy into it. Are you OK with that?"

"Yes, that will be fine, but I think we need to sit down sometime and do some future planning. Is it time to hire staff?"

Mackenzie pursed her lips, "Not now, maybe once we do our long-range plan."

"OK, let's do that by the end of the year. How does that sound?"

"That should work well. With all you have going on in your life, we need a deadline. Do you have any time for a personal life?"

Brock smiled, "As a matter of fact, I'm seeing a wonderful man I met at the garden centre. His name is Dirk." He explained their meeting and how he helped plant his tree but left out their other activities. "We've seen each other almost every night since we met almost a week ago. I'm getting used to having someone in my life again. How about you?"

She shrugged, "I've dated a few guys but none of them did it for me so I've accepted it will happen when the time is right."

"It'll happen when you least expect it! Look at me, I went to a client's home to plant a tree and I ended up with a boyfriend. Talk about customer appreciation!"

Mackenzie rolled her eyes, "Whatever you say Bro. I had better get going. She hugged him and left.

****

Making A Difference

Brock was getting ready for bed when Dirk's ringtone sounded, "Hello Dirk, what are you up to?"

"I'm lying here on my bed thinking about how wonderful this past week has been and I had to tell you."

"I feel the same way. We have spent a lot of time together this week and I think I'm going through Dirk withdrawal." Brock said with a chuckle.

"If that's anything like my Brock withdrawal, I feel for you. What are you doing right now?"

"I'm getting ready for bed, why?"

Dirk hesitated but responded with, "I have a bed."

"I know that only too well. What are you suggesting?"

"My bed is all warmed up and you could be enjoying the warmth within ten minutes if you come right now."

Brock caught the emphasis he put on 'come', "Are you serious? This is crazy."

"I'm a crazy kind of lonely guy. What do you say?"

"I say I'm getting dressed and I'll be there shortly. I just need to gather some things to take with me."

"The door will be open, just walk right in. I'll be waiting for you in my nice, warm bed."

*****

Brock turned the door handle and the door swung inward. The lights were out but the ambient light from the street allowed him to see where he was going. The bedroom was dark with a low light off to the side, but he could see Dirk's naked form walking toward him.

Dirk reached Brock and put his things down on the floor and proceeded to undress him in a playful orchestration alternating between buttons and small nibbles as skin became exposed. Brock got into the spirit quickly and Dirk led him to the bed. They fell as one and savoured each other's excitement.

They lay in each other's arms and Brock broke the silence, "That was wonderful. I'm glad you called."

Dirk smiled, "I'm glad I called. I manage on my own, but I love having you with me."

Brock had something on his mind and decided to get it out in the open, "We get along so well, and I love being with you. Is it too early to ask if you'll be my

Making A Difference

steady boyfriend? It sounds juvenile but I don't want to share you with anyone, in this way?"

Dirk looked into his eyes, "I haven't dated since Douglas, and this feels right. Yes, I'll be your monogamous boyfriend."

Brock did a fist pump. "YES! Dirk, I fell fast for you, and it scares me to think I have a boyfriend this quickly, but it does feel right to me."

"Let's plan to eat together as often as we can and if it isn't convenient some nights, we can just talk about it. We do have busy lives, but I want you to be part of mine."

"I'm good with all of this."

Making A Difference

Chapter 9

Kaleisha entered the kitchen with more energy than the guys had ever seen, and they would never have guessed it could be possible. Andrew needed to know, "You're overflowing, what's up?"

"We finalized the sale of my house for twenty thousand over the asking price. We can cut that amount off the mortgage you'll be holding for us. I'm ecstatic! They take ownership on the twenty-fifth, so I have three weeks to get things ready to move. Roger is as eager as I am and he's packing things already."

Both guys walked over to her and gave her a group hug, "Wonderful news!" Gregory whispered in her ear as they embraced.

"Are you guys going to be ready to move by then? I hope so because I need to move my stuff in here."

Andrew explained, "We guarantee we'll be ready, probably sooner than you'll be. Our cottage is almost ready so we can move our things there with minimal disruption to the guests staying here. It's furnished but we're getting rid of that stuff to make space for the move. We've been moving personal items over the years and some more when we knew the sale would happen. All we have left are the family pieces we identified during the sale discussion, our furniture from our private quarters, and several boxes of family Christmas decorations we packed in separate boxes when we took down Christmas last January. My hope is that we'll be cleared out of our space so you can move your things in. We're booking one of the guest rooms for our final days here so someone will be onsite if needed."

"Everything is falling into place, and I'll be the new owner of Mahogany Manor. I can't believe it! When I sent pictures home, they think I'm rich and I guess I am, maybe not in the money way, but in life ways. I have a blessed life. Thank you both for making this dream a reality for me."

The guys responded in unison, "We don't know anyone whom we would rather be the owner of Mahogany Manor. You'll make a great owner."

"Now, I have to get to work. How many for breakfast today?"

The guys filled her in on what needed to be done. They then left to go to the cottage. Their goal was to determine where the workers were on the timeline for completion.

Making A Difference

*****

Brock called Mackenzie and explained what the guys had told him about the time frame for the expansion, the safety measures that would be taken so that the residents could remain in the building during construction, and some management issues she would have to deal with. She asked questions for clarification and ended the call satisfied things wouldn't be too disrupted at the shelter.

The last day for applications for the therapist position was the day before and she reviewed the résumés for the eleven applicants. She determined she would interview all eleven and set up her calendar with hour-long appointment spots. She called them and negotiated a convenient 45-minute appointment for each. There were only two that needed a different day, so she felt good. She began to prepare her interview questions and called Marcy, one of her former professors at the university with whom she had become friends. She told her she was hiring a therapist and reviewed the interview questions with her. Marcy offered some improvements that would bring more information out for Mackenzie to consider. She also offered a couple of new questions and explained why she might want to add them. Mackenzie was pleased with the result and felt confident she could do the interviews. She had just ended the call when she heard a commotion and rushed out to check on things.

She found two teens in the lobby wrestling and punching each other. "Toby and Brian, what's going on here?"

Toby replied, "Brian stole my phone and I want it back."

Brian exploded, "I never stole any phone. I don't even have one myself."

"You were the last one down this morning and when I went to get my phone, it wasn't there." Toby started poking a finger into Brian's chest.

Mackenzie inserted herself between them and spread her arms to create a greater shield. "OK, Toby, where did you leave your phone?"

"I left it on the table beside the bed and it isn't there."

"Wasn't your room locked when you weren't in it?"

"I forgot. I know the rules say we have to but I'm only human, I forget sometimes."

"Have you called your number?"

"I can't, I don't have a phone."

Makenzie took her phone out. "What's your number?" She dialed it as Toby gave the numbers to her. A ringtone sounded from the living area. "Is that your ring tone?"

Toby looked puzzled, "It sounds like my ringtone but where is it?"

Making A Difference

As the phone rang, they followed the sound. Mackenzie needed to dial it again and they continued. As they walked between the chairs, the sound was coming from one in the corner. They felt down beside the cushion and pulled out a ringing phone.

Mackenzie looked at Toby, "How would your phone get in this chair? I remember you sitting in this very chair after breakfast and you seemed very taken with the new resident, Cherise. Could it be it fell down there during that time?"

Toby blushed, "Yes, I remember now."

"Do you have something you want to say to Brian?"

"I guess so.'

"Well, tell him."

"Brian, I'm sorry I accused you of taking my phone."

Brian nodded, "I accept your apology, but next time don't be such a dick."

Mackenzie looked back and forth between the two teens, "Follow our rules, lock your doors, and we shouldn't have any thefts. We'll always misplace things, but a phone is easy to sort out by calling it. Toby, I hope you learned a valuable lesson."

Toby hesitated while looking at the floor but looked up before Mackenzie had to remind him, "I learned a big one. Thanks for helping me find it."

"Ok, both of you go and do whatever you need and, in the future, come to me before you falsely accuse someone."

As they walked away together, Toby turned around and said, "Thank you Mackenzie."

*****

Mackenzie processed all the applicants and, using a grid of criteria she was looking for, narrowed the field to three. She called each for a second interview and booked time slots for the next day. She then made the calls to the other applicants and informed them they hadn't been chosen.

She called Marcy again and told her about the three seemingly equal candidates. She coached Mackenzie in how to dig deeper and suggested she look at their skills and expertise from different angles. When she ended the call, she felt a renewed sense of what she needed to do to help determine who would be the best choice for the shelter.

As each of the applicants arrived for their second interview, Mackenzie took Marcy's advice and made them comfortable with refreshments and warmer lighting from lamps on the side instead of the glaring overhead lighting. The goal was to destress them by creating a more friendly environment for the interview. It

Making A Difference

seemed to be working as one after the other came into the room and opened up to her. She noticed they were less formal in their answers, and she was able to have a good conversation with each one. At the end of the third interview, she thought about the information she was able to gather and when she compared the three, it was apparent who she would hire. She called each and gave them her assessment. Tom Remington was new in town and expressed his gratitude for having been chosen. He was eager to start, and they negotiated his first day would be the coming Monday.

She was wrapping up her day when she heard someone the front door. Cheryl, the lady who looked after the evening shift hurried by Mackenzie's office and greeted someone. Soon they were at her door. Cheryl explained that Emily, the teen was looking for a place to live.

"Hey Cheryl, Rhonna vacated her room today and won't be back but it isn't cleaned yet."

Emily spoke up, "If I can stay here, I'll clean the room myself if that's OK?"

Mackenzie didn't like leaving the cleaning to Emily but offered, "How about all three of us clean it. It shouldn't take long."

Marta smiled to herself. She loved Mackenzie's energy and her down-to-earth approach to her job. Since Mackenzie became the manager of the centre, she saw herself as one of the team. The job never went to her head. Cheryl added her voice, "I'm game."

Emily stepped up, "Show me where and I'll start."

"Marta, if you show Emily to her room, I'll get some fresh sheets and towels and be right up."

Marta looked at Emily, "Follow me. On the way we can pick up the vacuum, a mop and bucket, and some cleaners. Let me get the key first."

The three divided the work and in no time, they were standing at the door looking into a spotless room. Emily unpacked her backpack and put her few things away while Cheryl went to do her work.

Mackenzie offered. "You'll need to fill out some paperwork and we'll be done. "You travel light, do you have everything you need?"

Emily blushed, "I was kicked out of my home, and this is what I could grab minutes before I left. It wasn't pretty. Anyway, I've been staying with friends and managed to fill in the gaps with deodorant, toothpaste, toothbrush, and a few other necessities."

Making A Difference

"Let's go to my office and fill out the paperwork." Mackenzie led the way all the while explaining about the shelter, the responsibilities Emily had and the different programs the shelter offered.

As Emily sat, filling out the forms, she hesitated a little longer than Mackenzie expected, "Is something wrong?"

Emily looked up, "My name isn't Emily, but I don't want anyone knowing my real name because I don't want to be found right now. I want Mom and Dad to suffer a little, so they realize what they did. Mom is very much the mother...." Emily used her fingers to make quotes, "...and I expect she'll be upset. Dad figures he's right and will expect me to run home when life gets tough."

"We respect the residents' need for anonymity and anything told to us in confidence is never divulged. Your info is safe with us. You can be Emily here for as long as you want but I'd like to have your name and former address in case of emergency. Would you give me that information?"

Emily thought about this request, "As long as you do nothing with it unless there is an emergency." Mackenzie wrote her real name and her parents' names and address on a piece of paper she then slid into her desk.

They said their goodbyes and Mackenzie added, "Have a good night and I'll see you tomorrow."

"Thank you."

Mackenzie tidied her desk and left the shelter with a sense of purpose and a feeling Emily would make her home with them until she put her life back together. She reflected on hiring Tom and smiled as she thought about the new energy he would bring to the shelter workplace. She left and walked to her car thinking, '*Life is good*'.

Making A Difference

Chapter 10

All the new guests had checked in and Kaleisha was finishing off the last of the things she wanted to get done. She came down the stairs with an armload of dish towels, napkins, and placemats to store away. She saw the guys watching her, "You're staring at me, what's going on in your minds?"

"With things looked after, we thought we would take a drive out to see the progress on the cottage. Is there anything you want from us before we leave?"

"No, I'll just finish up before I leave, and I'll make sure I lock up."

"Great, we'll see you tomorrow morning, bye!"

Andrew and Gregory were interested in how the workers were finalizing all the last-minute tasks that needed to be done before the work would be complete. When they drove in the yard, Roy, the construction foreman was on his way to his car but rerouted to greet the guys with, "Are you coming for a look?"

Gregory smiled, "It's hard for us to stay away so, simple answer, yes. Can we go in?"

"I just locked up, come with me." He led them through the maze of construction materials and opened the door to let them in. "Since you're planning to live here fulltime, will this still be the cottage?"

"We decided it will always be the cottage and we want the feeling of carefree living that being on vacation always gives us. We decided we want to be on vacation the rest of our lives!"

"I like the sound of that" Roy swung the door in to reveal an open-concept living area with the living room, dining room and kitchen along the south-facing, almost-total glass wall overlooking the water. The walls and cathedral ceiling were encased in gleaming white shiplap which enhanced the vacation theme. The open concept continued at right angles to the kitchen to create a conversation area that also served as the office. The desk sits in front of a large window overlooking the forest of mature stand of maples and yellow birch. "We're ahead of schedule and expect to be completed in 3 days. How does it look?"

Andrew was standing looking out the office picture window marvelling at how alive it was with various forms of wildlife, "This is my favourite space. The windows overlooking the water are wonderful, but this window is simply magical.

Making A Difference

I'm going to start writing the books I've always wanted to but now I'm wondering if I'll be too distracted. I cannot think of a better distraction. I love it!"

"Aren't you glad we built this addition on?" Gregory said with a mischievous smile.

Andrew winked, "I'm so glad, and I might as well say it, you were right, again!"

Roy interrupted their reverie. He explained the things had to be done to call it finished and concluded, "Unless you have something we need to talk about, I'm heading home. It has been a long day! You can lock up when you leave."

Andrew looked at Gregory and they both shrugged, "I think we're good. Have a great evening!"

Roy left, closing the door behind him. They heard his car start up and drive away.

They were alone and Andrew cozied up beside Gregory and started planting soft kisses on his neck, "How do you feel about christening our soon-to-be new home?"

Gregory turned around and kissed Andrew on the lips and nuzzled his neck. He knew the exact spot, just behind his ear that drove him wild, and he intended on making that happen. He stepped back, "I'd be up for that!"

They chuckled and Gregory took Andrew's hand and led him out of the construction area to their bedroom. They felt free and alive!

*****

They got out of bed and as they collected their clothing, Gregory was pulling on his boxer briefs when he tripped, bumped into Andrew, and caused them both to lose their balance. They fell back on the bed and their ensuing laughter was rejuvenating! They heard a car door and stole a quick glance out the window.

"It's Stan and Oliver, quick, get dressed." Andrew whispered.

With arms and legs scrambling to put on the clothing, they heard Stan, "Hello, hello, we know you're here. Come out, come out wherever you are."

Andrew and Gregory tried to act put together and walked with purpose into the living area, Gregory explained, "We came today to check out things because we'll be moving here fulltime the twenty-fifth!"

Oliver walked over and picked up the shoulder seam on Andrew's T-shirt which he had put on inside out. With raised eyebrows he exaggerated, "I hope we didn't interrupt you two before the deed was done?" He winked.

Making A Difference

Gregory blushed, "You caught us. We thought we would christen our new, upgraded home."

Oliver added, "I knew it! I even said to Stan, as we drove in, that I hoped we would catch you in the act! I guess we just missed it but that's the story of my life." He looked around the space, The place is looking great! We have been stopping in regularly to check on the progress and talk with your hunky contractor. He wears his work boots so well, I almost swoon when I see them!"

"We're looking forward to having you as full-time neighbours. It can be quite lonely since most of the people come from May to October. How do you feel about how the place is turning out?" Stan, looking down the long room towards the kitchen.

"We're so glad we put this addition on. It gives the cottage a more open, sunny feeling. It's turning out just as we wanted it and we love the way it all fits together." Andrew stopped and then motioned them to follow him, "Come see this!" He got to the office area and stood in front of the window where the desk would sit. He half turned and swept his arm toward the view like Vanna White would do on Wheel of Fortune, "Isn't this the most wonderful view of the forest?"

Oliver couldn't hold back, "You live in the forest, what were you expecting?"

"Yes, we live in the forest but look at the forest floor and the birds, or dragonflies, or chipmunks or whatever. For me, watching nature is so peaceful." Andrew countered.

"You have been in the city too long. Look out any of your windows and you'll see the same thing."

"But this is where I'll be doing my writing and when I take a break, I have live entertainment." Andrew tried to explain.

Oliver couldn't let it go, "Live entertainment? Bring on the male strippers! Now that's what I call live entertainment. Think of the books you would be writing if that was your inspiration. I'd line up to read those!"

Stan stepped in to end the banter, "Andrew, this will be a wonderful place to write! So, when will this be ready for you to move something in? It looks almost done now."

"Two, maybe three days at most. Roy says there is a bit of trim and some painting to do. The kitchen counters are coming tomorrow and then they can hook up the plumbing. We'll move things a bit at a time and then have the moving truck bring the bulk of the furniture and artwork around the 23rd or whenever we can arrange it. Now that we've seen the place, we can schedule the move with more confidence."

"We look forward to having you living here!" Stan said with a smile. "Come on Oliver, we need to get those groceries home before everything melts."

Andrew and Gregory waved goodbye from the side entrance and watched as they drove off.

Andrew spoke first, "Well, that was a close call. I love that we got a chance to spend some time together. It has been a long time since I've felt so connected. I've missed having no pressure and the freedom to do what we want without worrying about guests."

Gregory looked at Andrew, "Me too. We let our day-to-day busyness get in the way of our spontaneity. I'm feeling like I did forty years ago! If this is what our retirement will be like, I can't wait! I love you!"

"I love you too. Let's catch the sunset before we leave. Too bad we couldn't stay the night."

"Soon, Gregory, very soon. Be patient and we'll be doing that every day."

They watched the sunset from colourful Adirondack chairs on the west-facing deck off the living room. They sat there and talked about what life would be like and revelled in the serenity of the evening.

Making A Difference

Chapter 11

Matthew walked into the office of The Counselling Group and gave his name and his scheduled appointment with Richard Paris. He then took a seat and looked for a magazine to read while he waited. A tall, neatly dressed, man with dark hair accented with grey at the temples came through the door, took a folder and called Matthew's name. He greeted Matthew and introduced himself as Richard Paris but asked him to call him Rich.

Mathew followed Rich into a sunny office with comfortable furniture and a large bookshelf filled with books of all colours, sizes, and thicknesses. It formed a colourful, abstract mosaic as a backdrop to Rich as he took his seat. Matthew took the overstuffed chair opposite Rich and waited.

"Matthew, I want you to feel comfortable and know that anything you say in this room stays between you and me unless you ask me to share something, or you disclose you want to harm to yourself or someone else. Do you have any questions before we start?"

Matthew went into pensive mode, "I had all kinds when I was trying to decide if I wanted to see a therapist, but my mind is blank right now."

"OK, what's going on that you decided you needed to see a therapist?"

"I really fucked up my life and I'm lost."

"When you say you fucked up, what does that mean to you?"

"I was in a relationship with Brock, one of the nicest people I've ever met. He loved me and I loved him, but I left him. I think I'm regretting my decision."

"When did you leave Brock?"

"Four years ago, when I went to Halifax to finish my degree to become an architect."

"You left him four years ago and you're just now thinking you regret your decision? Can you take me through your thinking that had you deciding to leave him?"

"I can try. We had been dating for four years starting in high school where we met and then through university here in New Brunswick. Brock had stayed in Saint John for his whole degree while I went to Fredericton after two years for another two years. I came home almost every weekend, and he was glad to see me, but I was missing something. When I was in Fredericton, I'd see all the cute guys and fantasize about them. I was loyal to Brock, but I started to resent I wasn't free. Going to Halifax meant I wouldn't be home very often, so I suggested to Brock we separate. We had had talks before, and I suggested an open relationship, but he didn't want that. He said if I wanted to see other guys he wouldn't stand in my way. I thought my lust over all the cute guys was working for me so, I ended our relationship."

"So, he wanted monogamy and you wanted open. After making that decision, how did life go for you?"

"At first I loved that the guys would hit on me or that I'd hit on them. I ended up having sex with many guys over the two years I was away. I don't even know how many and when a friend asked me, I guessed thirty but as I think about it, that number is low."

Rich had listened and he wanted to get Matthew thinking, "So, you're getting the sex you lusted about, how did that feel? Was it then you regretted your decision to end the relationship?"

Matthew sat pondering the question before answering, "How did it feel? Honestly, I was so caught up in my conquests, I didn't think about how it felt. I'd go from one guy to the next, sometimes I would have two or more in one night. Between my studies and the sex, I didn't have time to think so if I had any regrets, I wasn't aware. Maybe I'm in denial."

"I want to get a clear understanding of where your head was during this time. So, you sex your way through your Halifax years. Did you have any longer-term relationships or was it a series of short sexual encounters?"

"There were a couple of guys who I tried to have relationships with, but something was always lacking so I'd go back to having sex with other guys. I was open but I never told the guys in the relationship I was. I always practised safe sex and I use the Prep drug as an extra precaution."

"What happened when you returned to Saint John?"

"I brought Anthony, my latest attempt to have a relationship but that fizzled in a matter of months. Then I tried the scene here but again no long-term connections."

"Has Brock moved on?"

"I avoid contact and our common friends won't talk to me about him. I don't know if he has anyone in his life."

"I asked you before and you never answered, are you ready to answer now? When did you realize you regretted your decision to end the relationship?"

Making A Difference

"More lately than before. I went to see Brock and he was too busy for me. He owns Pine Valley Garden Centre, so I went there pretending I wanted to buy some plants. He had a lot happening there and had to leave. I felt that if I meant something to him, he would have made time for me."

"So, the regret you're feeling is a rather new feeling would you say? Can you tell me how you feel in general about your life over the past four years?"

"Everyone in my life is in a relationship and I miss all of the feelings that go with it. As for the past four years, I think I wasted my time because all that came out of what I did was the sex, and I must admit it wasn't as great as I imagined. For me, casual sex is missing the intimate emotional connection I had with someone I knew well. That connection just isn't there with someone I've just met. I regret losing the one person I had a strong emotional connection with, and I don't know where to go from here. That's why I said I was lost."

"Is this the first time you've analysed your feelings?"

"It is. I've not spent a lot of time figuring out why I did what I did. I think the best way to explain my behaviour is that I must have been running on a kind of sexual autopilot. I can't say I was happy in those four years, but I can't say I wasn't happy either. I guess I busied myself with my studies in Halifax, and when I returned to Saint John, I focused on getting our architectural firm up and running with my business partner."

They continued to talk but Rich found they were circling the same feelings over and over without breaking into deeper territory. It all seemed so superficial, and he wanted Matthew to dig below the surface to get at what motivated him to behave the way he did.

"Well, Matthew, our time is up for today and I want to thank you for being so honest. I have a good understanding of where you have been. I would like to see you weekly. How do you feel about that?"

Matthew was in a daze but shook himself out of it to respond, "If that's what I need to do, I'll do it."

Rich was pleased he would come back, "I feel we have only scratched the surface. In our next session I would like us to go down a layer to a deeper level. I'm hoping if we work through the levels, we discover why you went on your sexual autopilot. Can you spend some time over the next week to see if you can uncover what the next level might be?"

"I'll try but I'm not sure about anything anymore."

"I'll see you next week, same day, same time, and same place."

Making A Difference

*****

Matthew made his way home. He was still living at his parents' home to save the cost of having his own place. With the start of their business, there were lean times and he thought he would weather the storm in a safe place. When he asked his parents, they were thrilled to have him back with the knowledge he would be moving out some day.

His parents didn't understand why he broke up with Brock and he never shared any of his sexual exploits with them. They saw he wasn't the happy, energetic son who went off to Halifax but explained it away with all of the responsibility he had placed on his own shoulders.

He went to the kitchen and saw his parents, "Hi Mom, Dad, is there something I can help with for supper?"

His mother spoke first, "No, I think we have everything almost ready. Go clean up and when you come down the food will be on the table."

When he returned, supper was on the table. He sensed something was wrong. Both of his parents were quiet, and he noticed his mother's eyes were red like she had been crying. He became concerned, "Something is wrong, did something happen?"

They looked at each other and his dad spoke, "You know, I haven't been feeling well lately and I went through several tests to find out what's wrong. I got my results back, and they found a tumour in my bowel. When we hear tumour, we think of cancer, so I asked about my chances if the tumour was malignant. If it is, that cancer is treatable. If it's caught early, there's a high success rate. Mine isn't early but it isn't too late either, so they feel optimistic. I'll be going for surgery in a few weeks and then they'll discuss the course of treatment. Do you have any questions, Son?"

Matthew heard the words, and they were swimming around his brain. Questions? He had so many but none at the same time, "We don't have enough information for me to ask good questions. We won't have that until they get the results of the biopsy. How are you doing, Dad?"

"I've suspected something like this for a while, so I'm relieved we're finally going to get the information we need to sort out the next steps. Am I scared? A little, but I'm not investing too much into fear until I get more information. I guess I am afraid of the unknown."

His mother reached over and put her hand on her husband's hand. That simple, loving gesture had them all break into tears.

Making A Difference

Chapter 12

Mackenzie left early for the shelter to make sure she was there to greet Tom. When she parked her car, Tom got out of his and walked over to greet her. "I like to be early, but I wasn't sure when you would arrive. We seem to be on the same time schedule!" Tom said with a smile.

"I'm not usually here this early but I wanted to be here to greet you on your first day. Welcome aboard!" As he stood there, Mackenzie noticed his best feature was his smile. He was a little pudgy and his hair was an unruly mass of reddish curls. He had freckles and when he smiled, her heart melted, because he looked like a lost little boy. He had a boy-next-door demeanor about him that was so endearing.

They walked into the shelter and after getting some coffee from the kitchen, they sat in Mackenzie's office. She got him to complete the paperwork she needed to employ and pay him, and went over the policies, and procedures he needed to know. She then gave him keys for the shelter and said, "Come with me and I'll take you around and show you what keys fit where. They spent close to an hour viewing the shelter and property and explained that work would begin on the addition the next week. They went back to her office, and she shared what therapy she had been doing and he asked questions to help him understand his role.

She assured him, "We'll be overlapping for a while, but I want you to take over my client load. I'll ask if I could introduce you and then wean them off me and onto you. If there are any that do not want to move from me, I'll keep them, but I'm expecting most, if not all, will move over."

Tom nodded, "I'll follow your lead."

"We have a new resident who is here because her parents kicked her out. I know nothing more about why but she's here. I was hoping she could be your first client. I'll introduce you to her. Let's go out to the kitchen and see if she's around."

As they rounded the corner they almost crashed into Emily. Mackenzie seized the opportunity, "Hi, Emily. I want you to meet Tom Remington. Today is his first day as our new therapist. As part of your stay here, you'll have regular sessions with Tom. For your initial session, what time would work for you?"

Emily stood looking at Tom as Mackenzie spoke and after a few long seconds, "Hi Tom, I'm available all day today because I'm getting settled in. The sooner the better for me. When is your first opening?"

Making A Difference

Tom was surprised but pleased with her efficiency, "How about ten o'clock?" He looked at Mackenzie, "Unless there is something you need me to do."

Mackenzie shook her head, "You're doing exactly what I need you to do. Meet the residents on their terms." She looked to Emily, "Does ten o'clock work for you?".

"Great for me! Where do we meet?"

Tom pointed to the office next to Mackenzie's. "This is where we can start. After our first meeting, we could choose to use any of the conversation areas you would like, outside or inside."

"Ok, I'll meet you then, thank you. I have some things I need to get done. Bye." Emily was sincere and walked up the stairs to the resident floor.

Tom smiled, "I was wondering when I'd get to talk to the residents."

"I'm hoping you can meet a few more before ten. I want to get you known so when I suggest they work with you, it won't be a shock." Mackenzie started to walk, "Let's go into the kitchen and see who is there."

They were in luck with four more residents there eating. Mackenzie introduced him to one after the other, "This is Tom and today is his first day. He'll be taking over the bulk of the therapy sessions going forward so welcome him to the shelter." Each welcomed him and watched as he made the rounds with Mackenzie. By the time they had spoken with the four residents, two more came in and Mackenzie introduced them to Tom.

As they left to go to their offices, Mackenzie stated, "Seven down and three more to go. If we don't see them around, I'll book an appointment so you can meet them."

"I should go and prepare for Emily. How long are your sessions?"

"Usually, forty-five minutes but depending on availability I've had them go to an hour and a half if the resident needed the time. It really is your call. Whatever you're comfortable with."

Tom acknowledged he understood, "Thank you for the flexibility. See you later."

*****

Around one-thirty, Grant showed up with some trades people. He asked if it was OK to look around and decide on their plan of attack. She told them if they needed in a resident's room and the resident wasn't there, she would leave a note and they could view that room the next day. "We maintain their privacy."

Making A Difference

Grant thought about it and responded, "Maybe it would be best to schedule looking at the residents' rooms tomorrow afternoon. Today we'll do all the other areas."

Mackenzie looked at her dad, "That's fair, thank you. I'll put a note under everyone's door and I'll post the information in several of the common areas. We shouldn't have any issue viewing those rooms tomorrow."

Grant led his team around the building unrolling the drawings he carried under his arm and consulted them as he pointed out areas in the building.

When he was done, he went to talk to Mackenzie. She was in her office talking to Tom and Grant started to go in but veered away when he saw he was interrupting. Mackenzie called after him, "Dad, come in. Dad, this is Tom Remington, our new therapist. Today's his first day. Tom, this is Grant Matheson, my dad. He's also the general contractor for the addition. You'll see him around here a lot over the coming months."

Tom put his hand out to Grant, "Nice to meet you, sir."

"No '*sir*' greeting necessary, call me Grant."

"Will do, Grant."

'Dad, if you want to talk about the addition, Tom should hear things as well. If this is a family call, we're almost done here."

"I need to run over the tentative schedule so you'll know how the shelter will be affected." He told them the things they would see happening that week in preparation for the construction starting next week. "Once we begin the work, we should have weekly status sessions so you can keep everyone informed. They'll mainly involve safety concerns that we would like the residents to know about."

"What day and time would you like our update sessions to be? Let's say every Friday morning at nine o'clock. That way you have a few days to be able to communicate with everyone for the following Monday."

"Sounds good to me."

They said their goodbyes and he left Tom sitting in Mackenzie's office.

"Your dad seems really nice and very efficient!"

"He is on both counts."

*****

Tom was keen to keep busy and through his first week he would run ideas by Mackenzie whenever they connected. Mackenzie liked the way he thought and, the more they talked, the more she realized they had a lot in common. She started to look at him, not just as the shelter's therapist, but as someone she could call a friend. When he talked, he did so from his heart and was thinking of ways to help the residents. Because he was out in the common areas getting to know the shelter and its residents, they started seeking him out. Transferring some of the residents over to Tom was easier than she thought it would be and usually it was the resident who suggested the move earlier than she had hoped. By the end of the first week, he was scheduling sessions with half the residents.

On Friday, Tom poked his head into her office, "I'm done my first week, would you like to help me celebrate tonight?"

She tilted her head a little to the right and produced a mischievous grin, "I guess it depends on what you have in mind?"

"I thought we could go out for a drink and maybe grab some food. What do you say?"

"Sounds like fun. I thought I'd have a quiet evening by myself because the friend I was supposed to meet tonight just called to rebook. She wasn't feeling well and decided to stay close to home tonight."

They discussed the pros and cons of several places to go and realized they liked the same places and after a few minutes, they chose one.

"I want to go home and change first. I can meet you there."

Tom suggested, "How about I pick you up at six o'clock? Will that give you enough time?"

"That would be great. I only need another five minutes more to finish up here so six o'clock it is. Here's my address and phone number. I'd like to make one rule; we do not talk about the shelter. If it happens, the violator has to buy the other a drink."

"Agreed! I'm taking off, see you later." Tom waved and left.

Mackenzie sat doing nothing but thinking how nice Tom is and wondering if tonight would be a date or just two new friends getting together. She admonished herself for even thinking date and decided that simply being friends would be a good thing.

*****

While Mackenzie waited in the window for Tom to arrive, she scanned her small home. She bought it a year ago after saving for a year and living with her parents. Being just a block away from her parents and her brother was ideal, not too close. She never really worried about that because her parents never bothered Brock and he lived right next door. After she moved in, Brock picked her up and took her on a shopping spree as her house-warming gift from him. Having a rich brother certainly had its perks.

Making A Difference

Tom arrived a few minutes early, and Mackenzie was opening the passenger door before he could get out. "I had an idea you would be early." Mackenzie said with a smile.

Looking surprised, Tom asked, "What would make you think that?"

"Oh, I don't know. Could it be you were at the shelter every day before me this week and I was early?"

"Guilty as charged. I do not like to make people wait for me, so I arrive early. I've been this way all my life. Now, since you mentioned the shelter, I believe you buy my first drink, right?"

"Yes, I'll buy you a drink. I can't believe I violated my own rule within minutes!"

They got their table at the restaurant and when they ordered their drinks, Tom made sure the server knew Mackenzie was paying for his. "I wonder how many free drinks I'll get tonight?"

Mackenzie chuckled, "Enjoy that one because I'll not be paying for anymore!"

They talked easily and Mackenzie marveled at how easy it was for her to be with Tom. The conversation flowed throughout the evening, and they touched on many topics from their childhoods, schools they attended, favourite foods, music, even politics and religion. They finished their food and looked at the desserts. They decided to order one and get two forks. She never thought the evening would be this good.

Tom took a forkful of the 'Death by Chocolate Cheesecake', savoured it with almost too much enjoyment and said, "In all of our talking, you haven't mentioned a boyfriend or girlfriend; are you seeing someone?"

Mackenzie's mouth almost dropped open, but she had just taken a forkful of her meal and had to manage swallowing it before responding, "No, I did have a boyfriend, Ben, during high school but we parted ways during university. He's still a good friend, but we weren't couple material. I concentrated on my studies and after graduation I got the job I'm in, Notice, I didn't say where I work."

"As you started to say that line, I was waiting."

"You caught me once and that's it. How about you, anyone special?"

"No, there is no one special in my life at this time. It seems like I end up with girls who like bad boys and I disappoint. The longest relationship I've had was a year and when we broke up, she said that dreaded line I have heard so often: 'You're too nice.' I cannot be what I'm not." Tom punctuated his statement with a shrug.

"Well, I find your niceness endearing."

Making A Difference

"Mackenzie, I think you're delightful, and I hope this is the start of a great friendship. If it becomes more, I'd be open to that."

Mackenzie did her best to stifle her excitement with, "Well, let's just see where this friendship takes us."

Making A Difference

Chapter 13

It was Sunday Supper Day and as planned the Mathesons got together early to finish sorting through the last of Father Mike's boxes. Prior to arriving, Mackenzie and Brock agreed not to mention anything about the conversation they had last week about the journalist until the time was right. For that to be true, they needed a very clear understanding of what Father Mike had sent and they expected by the end of the day, they would know.

Everyone had their heads down and were sorting away when Brock broke the silence, "I was talking with Kaleisha, and she has everything in place to take over ownership of Mahogany Manor on the 25th. The guys will be moving to their enlarged cottage and from what they tell me, I guess it's going to be wonderful when it's completed. I can't wait to see what it looks like."

Grant added, "It looks like the guys will have a very comfortable place to live. A while back, they asked me to consult on what they wanted to do there, and I've been stopping out every week or so to see how it's going. Roy, a very capable construction guy, is handling the project and he will be finished a couple of weeks early. The guys will have no problem having their things moved in before the 25th."

Mackenzie held up a document, "I'm sure we had this Father Jacob Hamilton identified on a previous document, I just need to find it."

Martha added, "I've seen a Father Hamilton in some of the stuff I was reading. He seems to have been sent around to several parishes. It looks like he didn't mend his ways and the church failed the parishioners in those other dioceses. Our next step is to create a story out of all of this info and that's where we'll discover the repeat offenders." Today, her anxiety wasn't showing, and she seemed to be in a far calmer mood.

Grant reached deep into the box and brought out a group of documents. "This is the last batch. When we're all done processing the things we're now working on, we'll talk about our next step."

One by one, they completed their work and began talking to each other about what they thought the next step should be. Grant was last and the other three seemed to have agreed so they shared with him. They decided to document all the priest's names in a spreadsheet so they could sort by last name and first name so that all incidents of one priest would sort out together. They devised a simple coding

Making A Difference

system and Mackenzie began entering the records. They had maintained Father Mike's order so they decided to start coding that way so if, at any point, the documents got out of order and they needed to be placed back in that order, it could be done easily. Suppertime crept up on them, so Martha and Grant went to heat things up while Mackenzie and Brock processed through the piles. Brock would code the document and place it where Mackenzie could take it and input the information.

Martha stuck her head into the dining room, "Come to supper."

Sitting around the kitchen table they ate and chatted about whatever came up.

Mackenzie talked about the shelter and how well Tom was doing. She then added, "Tom invited me out for supper Friday evening, and I got to know him better."

Martha perked up, "Was it a date?"

"No, we decided we would work on the friendship. He's a nice guy and was fun to spend the evening with."

"Did he pick you up and drive you home? Who paid for the restaurant? Did you invite him in? How did you say goodbye?" Martha was on a roll and needed answers.

"Yes, yes, we each paid our own, yes, and we simply said we would see each other on Monday. That pretty well covers it. Oh, and if you want to know if we kissed, there was an awkward moment when I thought we would have, but we didn't."

Brock asked, "Did you talk shelter all night?"

"Actually, I made a rule before we left the shelter. We wouldn't talk about the shelter and if either of us did we would buy a drink for the other. I violated my own rule and bought him a drink. After that, I was cautious and thankfully I didn't screw up the rest of the night. He didn't screw up even once, so I bought all of my drinks and one of his."

Grant joined in, "Tom seems to be a nice man, at least in the few minutes I spoke with him, is he boyfriend material?"

Mackenzie's eyes opened wide and shot a glance at her father, "Dad! I would expect Mom to ask that question, not you! Well, since you asked, I see him as a definite candidate if our night is any gauge. He's like no one I've met before. He's a nice man, and an interesting conversationalist. I like him!"

Brock remembered something, "I've been meaning to tell you, but we've had so much going on that I keep forgetting. A journalist has been interviewing

Making A Difference

Andrew and Gregory about the activism they have done to bring about change in the LGBT world, most notably for same-gender marriage. Next year will the twentieth anniversary of it becoming legal in Canada."

Martha brought out, "They were on the front lines in New Brunswick for all gay equality issues. Any time a gay issue was being discussed, they seemed to be regularly in the paper, on the radio or TV, and taking the issues to Human Rights or to court. I think they deserve a book to be written about them."

"Kaleisha was talking about their contribution, and I thought we should look into an award they could receive. Maybe the Order of Canada, or the Lieutenant Governor's award, or one I don't even know about yet. I'm going to research it and apply."

'Brock, that's a wonderful idea. They have made a difference in so many people's lives." Mackenzie gave her brother a high five. "I'd love to sit and chat, but we have work to do. Before we leave this table, is there any dessert?"

Martha laughed, "You certainly squeezed that in effectively. Well, there is a banana cream pie if that works."

There was a scramble for dessert forks and a knife while Martha got the pie out of the fridge. When she brought it to the table, Grant took it from her hands, cut it with great precision, and served the plates. Everyone took one and savoured their first bite. "Mom, you have outdone yourself! When I asked if there was dessert, I never expected this delightful surprise!" They ate slowly and Mackenzie said, "It tastes like more" Everyone agreed, so Grant cut the remaining pie into four pieces and gave each one a piece. When they finished them off, she said, "Let's get back to work!"

Brock finished coding at 8:45 and Mackenzie entered the last record by 9 o'clock. When she sorted it, the end-product was what they were hoping for, and she printed out four copies. They agreed it was getting late, so they decided they'd each study the printout and come to next Sunday's Supper with recommendations about the next steps.

They hugged and said their goodbyes.

*****

On Monday, Brock parked in the driveway and, as he was getting out, Dirk came around the corner of the house, "Hi, while I was waiting for you, I walked around the gardens. It's my peaceful place. How was your day?"

Making A Difference

Brock walked toward him, and they hugged, "I'd like to walk your gardens with you. I had a good day but now that I'm seeing you, it has moved it into the great category!" He examined the gardens as they walked noting Dirk's handiwork in landscaping. It was evidence of someone with a love of gardening. He thought, *'Another plus!'*

"I've got Martha Stewart's Macaroni and Cheese in the oven. I've been craving it all day, so I decided that's what we're having tonight. I also made rolls to go along with it. Talk about carbs! It should be ready when we go in. Are you hungry?"

He responded, "I'm famished! How did you know that recipe is my favourite version of mac and cheese ever?"

Dirk smiled at Brock's enthusiasm, "I didn't but I've discovered that we seem to have similar tastes in food, so I'll be introducing you to all my favourites. Let's go in!"

They set the table and placed the casserole on a large trivet in the centre next to a basket of fresh rolls. They each took a healthy helping and savoured their first forkfuls.

Brock chewed and swallowed, "This is delicious! It's exactly what I remember it tasting like. You've done a great job, and these rolls are the best!"

Dirk was pleased, "Thank you. I agree, it's delicious if I do say so myself!" He laughed.

Dirk filled him in on his day which was slow on the work side but heavy on the domestic side. Brock had learned that he worked out of his office studio at the back of the house and communicated with clients and his team of developers around the world.

Brock filled him in on his day at the garden centre and was excited with something, "I've been thinking about developing the second phase for Pine Valley for a while and today, I made my decision. I'm going to pursue it!"

Dirk was intrigued, "What will the second phase entail?"

"The first phase was the garden centre, the green houses, and the storefront. The second phase will have an event pavilion, an art gallery, and a botanical garden with an arboretum. I want to use this project to allow people to buy memorial plaques for different areas of the gardens which will be connected to the event pavilion. It will be a great place for wedding photos."

Dirk was interested, "Do you have plans yet, and do you have the land?"

"I bought about one hundred hectares which is almost two hundred and fifty acres. Matthew and I talked about it over the years, and he designed the complete layout as a project for architect school. He gave it to me as a gift just before we broke up. He did a great job and I used it when looking for the land. I used ten hectares set for the garden centre. That includes, the green houses, the garden centre storefront, the parking area and I've set aside some land for future expansion should we need it. The rest of the land is for phase two. Pine Valley Garden Centre is running smoothly, and I feel it's time to grow the next phase. I'm excited!"

Dirk furrowed his brow, "Really? You hide it so well! My God Brock, you're almost vibrating as you talk about it. I'm excited for you too and if I can be any help, I'm here for you."

"I think I want to have Matthew update the design. I haven't talked to him in years but I hope he'll be open to doing this. I'll have to bite the bullet and go to see him."

Chapter 14

The movers arrived and Gregory walked them through *'the manor'* and pointed out the things they were taking. They were efficient and in under two hours all the items were packed into the back of the truck and ready to move to the cottage.

Kaleisha kept busy as the movers walked back and forth but joined Andrew and Gregory where they stood in the foyer watching the last of their things leave.

Andrew looked at Kaleisha, "Imagine, in two more days you'll own Mahogany Manor!"

She looked from one to the other and shared, "I'm so excited to have this opportunity, one I never thought was even possible. I'm sad you won't be part of my everyday life anymore. I know we'll see each other but it won't be the same."

Gregory teased, "Just pretend we've gone on a long trip, and you're looking after everything for us. Roger will be here living with you and before long you won't think of us at all. This will be yours so do whatever you need to do to put your personal stamp on it without giving any thought to *'what would Andrew and Gregory think about this?'* If you're happy we'll be happy, and anyway it will be your place, so it's nobody's business."

Andrew asked, "When do you think you'll be moving your things into your private space?"

"We have the movers coming tomorrow morning after breakfast when the guests have left for the day. Then we'll clean the house for the walk-through by the new owners the next day. I want everything to look great for them."

Gregory nodded and looked out the window, "Sounds like a plan. We had better get going so we'll be there before the movers arrive. We'll be back tonight to sleep so we'll see you later."

The moving truck left the driveway and the guys followed in their car. They made it to the ferry and were on their way over to the peninsula when the movers arrived. The guys knew the movers would catch the next ferry for sure. They had given the movers a detailed map and one of them was from the Kingston Peninsula and knew where it was so they felt comfortable they would get there.

They arrived in time to unlock, and block open the doors. To air the place out, Gregory opened some windows and let a cool breeze flow through.

Making A Difference

The truck arrived and the movers went straight to work. Before long, the furniture was in place, the labelled boxes were stacked in the corresponding rooms. The movers were paid, and they left Andrew and Gregory standing amongst their possessions.

They glanced around and then at each other. Gregory suggested, "Let's unpack the kitchen first."

Within two hours, the boxes were empty, everything was placed where they thought they should be, and they took a break. Gregory took a pitcher from the fridge and poured glasses of their famous Mahogany Manor Lemonade. They sat at the island and admired their work.

Andrew asked, "How do you like the way I had the movers arrange the furniture?"

Gregory laughed, "It's exactly where we decided everything should go and I think it fits so well. We're good planners! Let's hang the artwork."

Like the furniture, they had determined during their planning where specific pieces would hang. Andrew got the tool kit and as they brought out piece after piece, they measured and hung each one with great precision. Before long the open concept rooms looked like someone lived there. The last remaining boxes has lamps, lampshades, toss cushions, sculptures, and artifacts they had collected over their forty years together. The last thing they needed to do was to bring in the houseplants they had in their car.

The office furniture was in place and ready for use, but the internet wouldn't be connected until the next day. They were looking at all they had done when the door flew open and Stan and Oliver announced, "We're here with supper!"

Gregory rushed over to help them with their containers, "You didn't have to do this."

"I know we didn't HAVE to, we wanted to. You guys have been working here and we thought we'd take one thing off your mind." He was unpacking cooler bags and setting things out on the counter.

Andrew watched and gave a low whistle, "Look at all of this food, thank you, guys! Thank you! I am famished."

Oliver removed the covers off the dishes, "We didn't know what state things would be in because of the move, so we decided to have an indoor picnic. Dig in, everything is ready to eat!"

Gregory rubbed his hands together, "I'm ready too. Andrew, you do the plates and glasses. Stan, you get some cutlery from this drawer, and I've got the napkins."

Making A Difference

In no time, the table was set, and the containers placed in the middle. They dug in. Conversation was spirited and Oliver was entertaining the table with his dry, sarcastic wit, and laughable impersonations.

"So, you seem to be settled in and it looks like you live here so when do you move in for good?" Stan asked as he looked around the place.

"Today was the main move so Kaleisha would be able to move her things in tomorrow. She takes ownership the day after tomorrow and that's when we move here for good." Andrew explained.

Gregory added, "We'll be living out of a suitcase in one of the guest rooms for tonight and tomorrow night. Tomorrow, we'll manage the B&B while Kaleisha looks after her move. She takes ownership the next day so after she signs the papers with the lawyer, we'll leave there and come here. Before then, we have to get a big grocery order and remember to put some things we have forgotten at '*the manor*', in our car. For the most part, we think we have everything we need to be comfortable. Time will tell."

*****

The guys felt funny waking up in Scarborough Fair, the guest room on the first floor. They showered and tidied the room before going out to the kitchen. Kaleisha wasn't coming in until the movers were finished clearing out her place, so Andrew was looking after breakfast and Gregory was going to meet the internet installer at the cottage.

Gregory kissed Andrew and took the last few items they found when they looked around the B&B for things they had forgotten. As Gregory drove, he marvelled at the changes they were going through and thought about what retirement would be like. They had talked about retirement many times, but it was always out there somewhere in the future and now it was here. He parked beside the deck and started unloading the car and carrying things into the cottage. They always called this place the cottage and they said they would continue after it was their home. '*Cottage*' sounded so restful so he hoped it would remain. He had just taken the last load in when the installer's van rolled into the driveway behind his car.

The installer got out. He was a good-looking twenty something young man with tight jeans and a black T-shirt which clung to his well-developed abs. He asked, "Hi, my name is Neal, is it OK to park here until I finish?"

Gregory wasn't going anywhere until he was done so responded. "Hi Neal, I'm here until you're done."

As they walked into the house, Neal asked, "Are you Andrew Wallace?"

Making A Difference

"No, he's my husband, but my name should also on the account, Gregory Allen."

"Alright, I see your name here as well. OK, where's the electrical panel?"

Gregory led Neal to the panel, and they discussed where he would like the modem to be installed. After a bit of discussion, they decided on a central spot and Neal went to work.

Things were going well. Neal was back and forth to his van and was hooking things up. When he was ready, he asked what password Gregory would like instead of the string of letters and numbers. He chose one and Neal had it working in short order. Gregory tried his iPad, and announced he was able to connect. Neal disappeared into the panel area.

Gregory was busying himself with emails when he heard Neal clearing his throat. He turned around Neal was standing waiting, but Gregory wasn't sure why. He could see Neal was nervous, "Neal, you don't seem comfortable, what can I do for you?"

Neal hesitated, "I'm sorry, I don't want to bother you, but you said you had a husband. I thought you could help me."

Gregory heard pain, "Come over here and sit for a bit. How can I help you?"

"I think I'm gay, but I don't know any gay people. How do you know when you're gay? I'm so confused."

"You know you're gay when you're attracted to someone of the same sex. Are you attracted to men or women?"

"Women are nice, but I love men. I get all excited just being in the same room with a guy and I fantasize having sex with him. I think about men all the time, but my family is very conservative and have negative things to say about gay men, so I have to fight those things all the time."

"Have you ever been with a man?"

"No, I've always been afraid to do anything, but I felt safe being here with you. I've seen a bit of porn and I know I want to be with a man. In those movies, I see couples accepting another guy in. Do you and your husband do that?"

"My husband and I do not have an open relationship. I'd suggest you look for someone who you can become friends with and who you can have sex with. You're a very good-looking man so you shouldn't have any trouble finding someone."

"I'd love to meet someone but how? I don't trust those dating sites, how would I know I wouldn't connect with someone who knows my family?"

Making A Difference

"I understand that fear. We were in the closet for years because of what our families would do if they knew. Did you ever think that whoever you met, was also on a gay hook-up site so they have nothing to use against you?"

Neal thought, "I never looked at it that way. Where can I meet guys?"

Gregory wondered if he should offer, then asked, "Neal, I have some young friends who I think would like to be your friends. If it goes anywhere after that, it would be up to you. How would you feel about meeting some of them?"

"I'd like that. Could we meet here? I feel safe with you."

"How about we have you out for supper with some of our young, close friends. Probably no more than six, but I think you need to start out small."

"That would be great. You could text me when you have the plans finalized. Here's my number."

As they walked out to the van, and said their goodbyes, Neal said, "I hope to see you soon."

Chapter 15

Carson found his way to Andrew and Gregory's cottage. As he walked up the stairs, he took in the breath-taking scenery. Andrew met him at the door, and they talked about the views. "Come in and see the views we have from our living space."

Carson looked across the open concept and then noticed, "Hi Gregory, you guys have an amazing view from this area. I think I'd never leave."

Gregory spoke up, "We love being able to look out and enjoy it. What we haven't gotten used to is not going into the city every other day. Now that we don't have the B&B we have so much more free time."

Carson smiled, "Good, now I can step up my interviews. With the new timeline, I'm ready to flesh out the stories you told me about that weren't necessarily in the media." He dug through his briefcase and brought out a few sheets of paper, "I have these activities, but I want to know other things that were going on. I believe the activities that helped gain equality were the foundation to same-gender marriage becoming legal. We won't get into detail today, but we'll later. Right now, let's get what I'll call the signposts. What are some of the first things you did or were involved in that added to the way people or government viewed gay people?"

The guys sat back and thought. Gregory was the first to speak, "I think things started to open up for us when we came out. Prior to that, the fear of losing our family and friends, our jobs, and having to suffer discrimination against who we were, kept us out of the public eye. We felt we couldn't participate in any of the activities. Once we came out, we started fighting for equality. I think our first activity was when Andrew took our workplace to task over benefits for LGBT employees. It took about a year to win that one."

Andrew joined in, "Our next piece of activism was when we lodged a Human Rights complaint against the Federal Government because they discriminated against us in our Registered Retirement Savings Plans investments. If there was a death of a partner, our investments would have to be de-registered but for straight couples, they retained registration and their investments were rolled over into the name of a surviving spouse. That took several years to win."

Gregory added, "And there was the time we lodged a complaint against our Member of Parliament for refusing to meet with any members of the LGBT community to talk about rights but who openly welcomed Christian groups in for a

Making A Difference

talk. We lost that one, but the media covered some of it and people got to use their own reasoning to judge whether it was discrimination. The Human Rights group deemed that the person is elected, and it could be handled at the polls. I, personally, think they were wrong because a marginalized group didn't have the power to oust any politician, especially in what was then a very conservative-minded riding."

Andrew took another turn, "We also lodged a Human Rights complaint against the Mayor when she refused to allow the gay community to have a float in the Christmas Parade saying, *'There is no room for sex in the parade.'* We met with the mayor and laid out our case which changed her mind for future parades, so we let that complaint die. In 2003 when the same Member of Parliament got up in the House of Commons spouting homophobic things about gay people, we started the first Gay Pride Parade in Saint John. That was a scary but exhilarating time for our movement."

Gregory added, "There were lots of negative opinions during that time and it seemed like they were the only Letters to the Editors that were being written. To counter the negative comments, we joined a host of others to respond laying out our world in very logical terms. There were a lot of very narrow-minded religious people who were concerned for our soul but very few got beyond the Bible to be concerned about our lives."

Carson thought it was a good thing he was recording the interview because as hard as he tried, he couldn't take detailed notes. He would have to augment his notes with what was recorded. "I'll look at the Letters to the Editors over a number of years to get a feeling for what was being said and the responses to those letters as well. That will certainly flesh out the timeline."

Andrew remembered something, "We also started PFLAG meetings in 1996. A mother of a gay son came to me and asked if I'd help her start up a Saint John meeting. I knew very little about what this involved but that never stopped me before, so we got the word out and the first meeting had sixteen moms and dads as well as a few gay and lesbian individuals. We ran those meetings until we passed it over to Grant and Martha. In an effort to organize nationally, PFLAG Canada was formed, and I became the first Executive Director. Together with the Chapters across Canada, we developed support material and the organization has grown from there."

"Now that you say that, we should mention the organizing of Pride week and the awareness that provided. When I look back at the first Pride Parade and the activities that were planned in subsequent years, the information got out to the public and caused discussions. People on both sides got into conversations and one-

Making A Difference

by-one people's minds began to evolve. Another event was the National Day against Homophobia and Transphobia that we supported." Gregory energized as he spoke.

Andrew jumped in, "We can't forget all of the support groups we started and/or supported to allow people to discuss their issues in a non-judgemental environment. Many of these were born of a need from one person and we brought together many people to get the diverse views. At one such meeting, a co-worker walked in, looked at me and said "Now you know" but I didn't know anything other than a co-worker had walked in. What I didn't notice was that he was dressed as a woman. That was the first of many connections and he was in transition from a male to a female at a time when there wasn't a lot of information available. I asked if he would do a presentation so we could all learn. He did an amazing job and I learned so much. I offered to support him/her anonymously when he needed to dress as a female for the two years before her surgery."

Carson looked at his list and decided he would drill down on these items another day. He asked the guys to put an approximate date on each of the items so he could place it on the timeline. Andrew and Gregory took each of the items and discussed when it happened. They even wrote the things out on separate pieces of paper and manually arranged them. As they would land on an order they discussed if they had the order correct. They finally settled on an order and told Carson that that was the best they could do.

*****

It had been a long night. Carson was listening to his recording and reviewing his notes from the today's interview with the guys. It was a particularly newsy day. The more he interviewed them, the more information he found out that wasn't part of the original timeline he had researched. He started out thinking the timeline would be the outline for the book. Now, he was feeling like his process had gotten out of hand and he seemed to be all over the place. Prior to meeting with the guys, he researched media and believed the news items he had found were defining the journey the book would document. What he was finding out during his time with the guys is that one conversation would lead to several items that he hadn't heard about. He realized the project was bigger than he had expected and not everything got in the news.

He decided to come at this from a different perspective. He needed to create a new timeline which included all the items that he didn't have in the old one. He would do this by, documenting the items that come out in their stories and try to date them for the timeline.

Making A Difference

He had talked to his publisher after today's interview with the guys and explained the situation. He proposed how he was going to handle it, and, promising a more complete history, he got the greenlight for a more evolved book. This would mean the story would be about Andrew and Gregory. They would form the core of the book and he would fill in around them with the other players. He hoped he could sell this new format to them tomorrow when they meet.

*****

Carson went to the cottage to introduce the change he had OK'd with the publisher. "Andrew and Gregory, every time I interview you, I'm finding you have a wealth of information and activities I believe I need to include in the book. I want us to work together to flesh out a timeline that connects with your life and goes beyond what was reported in the media. I've spoken with the publisher, and they have agreed to make the book about your journey and include all the other players as part of what you were involved with whether you were the creator or instigator or a supporter of someone's else's initiative. Will you go along with this new approach?"

Andrew leaned forward, "So, if I hear you correctly, you want the story to be about our involvement."

Carson nodded, "Yes, you would be the central core and we would add others as we need them. To tell an accurate story, we include everything that hit the media on the LGBT equality story whether you were the main characters or supporters or a bystander. We would tell the story from your perspective honouring everyone's contribution in bringing about equality, especially how same-gender marriage became legal in New Brunswick."

Gregory commented, "So, the story would detail our role in helping make this happen and include the others who were part of it."

Carson let out a slow breath, "I would even give you first review before the publisher sees it to guarantee that you're OK with how the story is unfolding. Even when someone else is in the forefront, I'd write about how you personally perceived what was happening and how you felt about it."

Andrew listened intently and added, "I like that we can have first review and I like that you'll keep the accuracy with others who were in the front as well. Yes, we did a lot, but others contributed as much or more than we did."

"So, am I hearing you're OK to proceed with this new plan?" Carson raised both eyebrows waiting for their answers.

Making A Difference

Andrew sat back, more relaxed than he had been, "Yes, I'll agree to proceed but we must have first preview."

Gregory was nodding, "I agree to proceed."

Carson smiled, "Thank you, guys. This will be a more accurate book than I could have done without you. So, the first thing we need to do is flesh out the timeline with the things you were doing, feeling, supporting, and encouraging outside of what was being reported in the news. This will give us a more complete history. Let's get to work."

Chapter 16

Andrew and Gregory worked at the manor while Kaleisha went to the lawyer to sign the papers that made Mahogany Manor hers. She returned with Roger and filled the guys in on what had happened.

Andrew added to her story, "We signed the papers yesterday and our lawyer will be delivering us a certified cheque representing your down payment minus their fees and any disbursements. It looks like the manor is officially yours!" They had put together a tray with glasses and a bottle of chilled champagne. "Let's toast this wonderful achievement!" He opened the bottle and poured the four glasses and handed them out.

Holding his glass up in the air, Gregory started, "To Kaleisha, the most gracious new owner of Mahogany Manor. May your life here be as fulfilling as the life we had here."

Everyone clinked their glasses together with a "Here's to Kaleisha!" and took a sip.

Each person took a turn with Kaleisha being the last, "Here's to Andrew and Gregory, the most wonderful bosses I've ever had. Thank you for your support in making this dream become a reality!" She held up her glass and everyone clinked. "Here, Here."

Roger stood apart and looked at the other three, "I remember the day I came here for the first time. When this beautiful woman opened the door with her infectious smile, my heart took a jump. I was left without words and when I went to speak, gibberish came out." He looked at Kaleisha, "You laughed and asked if I wanted a room. All I could manage was a nod. That day, I knew I wanted you in my life, but it took you a bit longer to see me in a different light. That was three years ago in the middle of the pandemic. I found a safe haven here and, over several months, you finally agreed to be my partner. I love you Kaleisha!"

Kaleisha blushed, "Roger Hunter, you're a crazy old fool." She grabbed a dish towel from the counter and swatted Roger with it and then fell into his arms.

"Crazy enough to want you in my life forever." He dropped to one knee and held an open ring box up to her, "Kaleisha, my darling, will you take this crazy old fool to be your husband?"

Making A Difference

"Yes, a thousand times yes!" She took the ring and slid it on her finger. She pulled Roger up and kissed him.

Andrew looked at Gregory and he nodded, "Kaleisha, Gregory and I would like to give you your reception as your wedding gift. You could have it here and we'll manage all the food. How does that feel to you?"

She lit up, "Thank you! I've dreamed of getting married here, I just never thought my dream would come true. If I can ask one more favour, if Mom doesn't want to give me away, I would like you to play father of the bride. I'll ask Mom, but she's so shy and traditional, I know she'll say no because she wouldn't want to be the centre of attention."

"I'd be honoured. I can step in at any time so if your mom does say no but has a change of heart I can easily step aside. The important thing is you get what you want."

"Thank you, Andrew! You're the closest father figure I have in my life."

Roger looked to Gregory, "Would you be our master of ceremony?"

"Yes, Roger, I'd be honoured."

Kaleisha added, "I'm going to ask my daughter, Alvita to stand up with me. Roger is going to ask my son, Winston to be his best man. We have lots to do!"

*****

On the way home from Pine Valley, Brock stopped in to see Kaleisha. He walked in the foyer and found her in the kitchen, "Hello owner of Mahogany Manor Bed & Breakfast! How are you feeling?"

"It hasn't completely sunk in yet, but I had another surprise today. She held out her hand and wiggled her fingers. Brock took several long seconds to catch on but then he saw the diamond, "Roger proposed to me, and we're going to get married right here in my new home. The guys have offered to do our reception as a wedding gift. I'm bursting I'm so happy! And, wait for this, Andrew has agreed to give me away, and Gregory has agreed to be the master of ceremony."

Brock picked her up and swung her around, "Congratulations! I'm so pleased for you!"

They laughed and talked about things she had been thinking about for the wedding. "Remember you told me about the valentine wedding with and all the red roses and the garlands everywhere? I want the same decorations for my wedding. Could you do that for me?"

Making A Difference

Brock smiled, "I've never done anything like that, but I watched the team decorate the place, so I'll say yes and make it happen for you. That will be my wedding gift to you."

She threw her arms around Brock's neck and hugged him without letting go for a long couple of minutes.

Brock looked at her, "Follow me." He took her out to the front hall where a large box was sitting. It was wrapped in beautiful floral paper with a large bow. "Kaleisha, I've wanted to give this to you for a long time but waited for the right moment. On your first day of you owning this place seems like the right time to me. Go ahead, open it."

Like a child on Christmas morning, she ran over and tore at the paper. When she exposed the box, she still had no clue but that didn't stop her from yanking on the flaps and got it wide open. The tissue was plentiful, and she dug around until she touched something hard. "I don't know what it is yet, but I know where it is." She gingerly separated the sheets of tissue and exclaimed, "Just like my Robbie." She brought out a tall crystal parrot with many vibrant coloured feathers. Where did you find this?"

"I remembered seeing it at a gallery I visited and when you showed me a picture of your pet parrot, I knew you were getting this as a gift. I thought the colouring is very similar to the picture."

Kaleisha started crying, "It's very close. When I look at this I think of Robbie. I'll have a special place in my private quarters. I'll place it in the living area window and let the sun reflect the colours onto the walls. I love it! Thank you so much! I have my special tea steeping; will you have a cup with me?"

Brock looked at his phone, "I have half an hour so yes, I'd love to have one."

Kaleisha had the tea ready and on the table along with a plate of sweets. "I knew you would be by today, so I made your favourite square. Dig in!"

Their chatter got onto the topic of the award Brock was looking into and he told her he had completed the forms on the website and got acknowledgement that they had been received. "Now, I wait!"

Kaleisha had a sparkle in her eye as she looked at him, "Brock, you do not seem as sad as you have been, have you met someone?"

Brock blushed, "I can't hide anything from you. I've met someone, Dirk, a wonderful widower around my age. He hasn't dated since his husband died but we've had three dates and we're going out again tonight. He showed up one day while I was moving trees around in the side lot. He was looking for one and I delivered it. The rest is history. I really like him."

"Have you told anyone?"

"No, you're the first. I want to make sure we're compatible before I introduce him to everyone." He looked at the time and drained the rest of his tea. "I have to run; I don't want to keep Dirk waiting." He kissed Kaleisha's cheek and left.

*****

Brock reached for his phone, "Hey Andrew, we haven't connected in ages. What's up?"

"We're moved into our cottage and wondering if you would be interested in coming for supper on Thursday at 5:30. Neal, the installer who hooked up our internet is in his mid-twenties and wants to come out but doesn't know how to meet people. We thought we would invite a few guys over so he could meet people his age."

"Please don't tell me this is a set-up, Andrew. I've met someone and would like to introduce him to you and Gregory. Maybe we could both come for supper."

"This wasn't meant to be a set-up but if something happens with one of the guys and Neal, I wouldn't blame them. Gregory tells me he's nice and quite handsome! Congratulations on dating someone. Does he have a name?"

"His name is Dirk and we met at Pine Valley." Brock filled Andrew in on what they have been doing and that he was on his way to meet him."

Andrew smiled but then got somber, "Brock, feel free to say so but would you mind if we invited Matthew to supper as well. I won't if it would bother you."

Brock thought about seeing Matthew again, hesitated and after a few, long seconds, "I think I'll be OK if he is. It's been four years, so we need to break the ice that separates us. Yes, go ahead and invite him. I want us to be friends, and this might be the way to go about it."

Andrew was surprised with the positive tone to what, in the past, would have been a sensitive topic, "As long as you're sure. I thought we could also invite Henry and Jeremy."

"It would be good to see them again. So, Thursday at 5:30, is there something we can bring?"

"We have the menu planned but, if you wanted, you could bring a bottle of wine."

"Great, see you then! I'm looking forward to seeing what you've done with your cottage."

Making A Difference

"We are looking forward to seeing you and meeting Dirk."

*****

When he went to Dirk's place after work, he filled him in on the supper invitation at Andrew and Gregory's cottage.

Dirk smiled, "So, you're ready to introduce me to your friends."

Brock grinned, "Yes, I'm ready. The only caution I have is that Matthew, my ex, will be there. They asked me if I minded him being there and if I did, they wouldn't have invited him. This will be the first time we'll both be at the same social event. I think it's time."

Chapter 17

Stan and Oliver walked into Andrew and Gregory's living area from the deck, "Honey I'm home." Oliver yelled out to the empty room. "If you're not decent, get decent, we're here to visit."

Andrew came out from behind the kitchen, "Hi Guys!" He went over to greet them and explained Gregory was having a nap.

Stan lowered his voice, "Well, he was until Oliver bellowed, I'm sure he's awake now."

As Stan finished his sentence, Gregory appeared in the hallway outside their bedroom, "No need to whisper, I'm awake."

They sat and chatted the afternoon away. "Wow, look at the time! Why don't you guys stay for supper?" Andrew asked.

They were setting the table and laughing as they reminisced about a party that Stan and Oliver had at their place last summer.

Oliver explained, "Some of those guys are simply crazy and proved it when they stripped off and cannon-balled into the water. The best part is when an old couple slowed to see what was going on only to find a dozen naked men standing on the dock. I think they were looking for a specific property, but they got a whole lot more than they bargained for and sped off." He finished just as his phone sounded. "Excuse me, it's my brother." Oliver went to the far end of the living room and over the next ten minutes it was clear through his animated conversation was getting exasperated.

Andrew asked Stan, "Is something going on with his brother? Oliver seems agitated."

"His mother isn't well, and his brother always tries to put a guilt trip on him. It really upsets him he can't go visit her but we just don't have the money to up and fly anytime and his brother could easily afford it but he wants to make Oliver feel inadequate."

Oliver hung the phone up and had tears in his eyes, "He pisses me off so much and accused me of not loving our mother. I'll be damned if I have to admit I don't have the money to go. He had ridden my back all these years about being just a waiter when I could have made something of my life. He's so fucking religious, he continually reminds me I'm going to hell. Well, to hell with him!"

Making A Difference

"Does visiting your mom cost much?" Gregory asked.

"It's really the circumstances that cost. One thing is I'm too stubborn to be beholden to my brother. Mom lives in a nursing home and the only place to stay is his place and use his car to get around. I'd have to be breathing my last breath to end up there. I'd feel like I'd be on display. So, I would need plane tickets, a hotel, meals, and a car. I'd like to stay more than a couple of days, so it's completely out of the question."

Gregory understood, "I see. Don't you hate it when family isn't supportive? I have a sister who can't even visit our home because her church family doesn't agree with us being gay. Don't get me going because we were so close growing up and now, she can't come visit because of a group of bigots whom she lets rule her life."

Oliver nodded, "I guess you can understand my situation. I hate it! Now, let's lift our spirits and by spirits, where is the wine? I'm going to need a whole bottle myself!"

*****

Brock was pacing in his Pine Valley office. He wanted to call Matthew but thought he should go to Erb & Wilder Architects in person. He walked out of his office and spoke to the centre manager, "I'll be out for the next couple of hours. If you need me, I'll have my phone."

Driving there, he admonished himself for not calling to see if Matthew had some time to talk but he decided that if he didn't today, he would make an appointment for later. Calming himself down, he parked, grabbed the drawings, and walked in. He explained to Sheila, the receptionist, that he wanted to see Matthew about a design. She told him to have a seat, asked if he wanted a coffee and disappeared around the corner when Brock said he was fine. He could hear murmuring but couldn't make out any of what was said. Sheila returned, "Matthew will see you now, please follow me." She led him to Matthew's office and announced his arrival.

Matthew stood and came around the desk. He gave Brock his hand to shake but Brock responded, "Is a hug out of the question for two friends who have drifted apart?"

Matthew's face broke into a huge smile and threw his arms around Brock, "Oh Brock, I'm so glad you have made the first move. I caused us to part and never felt I could discuss being friends."

Making A Difference

"Let's put the past aside and become the friends we were, before we were boyfriends. I've missed you."

They heard someone behind them, and both looked to the door where Anson stood. He commented, "Well this is a sight I had hoped would happen years ago. Better late than never! How have you been Brock, I haven't seen you around."

"I've been so busy with Pine Valley and putting all my spare time to get it running smoothly. Now I want to do phase two, so I thought Matthew had to be the architect." He looked at Matthew and said, "What do you say?"

"Yes, I would be proud to be your architect." and thought, *'I want to be your everything'* but said, "Brock, Pine Valley is turning out just like you talked about which, of course, is what I used to do your design."

"Did the guys invite you to supper on Thursday yet?"

"They left a message and I've been considering it, but I was concerned about you being there, so I hadn't responded. Now that we've become friends again, I'll let them know I'll go."

Brock turned to Anson, "Would you and Charles like to come to supper on Thursday?" He explained about Neal and how he wanted to meet gay men their ages.

Anson checked his calendar, and they were available.

"Let me call Andrew." Brock put one finger up for Anson to pause and made the call. Andrew picked up, Brock explained the situation, and asked if Anson and Charles could attend. He hung up and turned to Anson, "You're in!"

Matthew was looking at the time, "I have an appointment in an hour, so we had better get to work. Let me see the drawings." He unrolled them and reviewed the design. "So, Brock, what ideas do you have?"

Brock said goodbye to Anson and started pointing things out on the drawing, "I have lots of land and I want the event pavilion to exist on its own with the botanical gardens in the rear and closer to the garden centre. The arboretum could be at the back of the property next to the botanical gardens. I want lots of pathways, statuary, and fountains. There is a lake I want to showcase behind the pavilion and incorporate it into the gardens. I want a meandering drive lined with trees as the approach to the pavilion so it cannot be seen from the road. The parking lot should be surrounded by green spaces with trees and bushes and enough parking for 400 cars to cover the event pavilion and the people to tour the gardens and arboretum. The art gallery should be connected to the pavilion on one side with a separate entrance. The pavilion should have windows overlooking the lake and gardens and be equipped with a bar, a coat check, and a great kitchen."

Making A Difference

"Well, you have really thought about this. Let me take this design and see if I can get you everything you want. You certainly have the land so I'm feeling anything you want should be able to be encompassed in the new design. I hope I'll have something within a week. I'll call you. Do you still have the same cell number?"

"Yep, you can call me on that. Thank you for doing this." Matthew walked him out and watched him as he got in his car and drove away. His appointment wasn't with another client, but with his therapist.

*****

When Matthew arrived, Richard Paris was in the reception area talking with Penny, his receptionist. He acknowledged Matthew and asked him to take a seat in his office, "I'll be in shortly."

Matthew sat waiting and thought about seeing Brock and what he hoped it would mean. He was sitting smiling when Rich joined him.

"You look a lot happier today than you were in your last visit, what has caused your smile?"

Matthew explained Brock's visit and how he felt about it, "I've been hoping we could be friends again and today, he told me he wanted our friendship back."

Rich saw something more, "When Brock says friendship, what does that mean to you?"

"Things will go back to the way they were. We'll start out as friends and hopefully it will lead to us getting back together."

"Do you think this will solve your feeling of being lost?"

Matthew thought, "If I have Brock back in my life, I won't be lost any longer and the regrets go away."

Rich tried to keep a neutral look on his face, "You didn't know if Brock had moved on last week so what if he has?"

Matthew was silent for a long time, "I never thought about that. I guess I'd still have the regrets and I'd feel lost again. Just saying this makes me think I've set off alarms in your head."

Rich smiled, "You certainly have a way with words. I'm concerned you haven't looked inside to solve your issues. Today, you are looking to Brock, and I don't think your issues can disappear that quickly. Would you say you're dependent on others for your view of who you are?"

"What do you mean by that?"

Making A Difference

"Well, last week you said you loved the attention from the guys who hit on you, but you didn't feel fulfilled. You said there was a void and the only person who filled that void was Brock. I'm concerned that if he has moved on and only wants a friendship, it will not be enough for you. I want you to validate yourself and not seek validation from others. Were you bullied in school?"

"All the time. That's how I met Brock." He told him his story and how it led to a relationship.

"So, you got the message from the bullies that you were not worthy of friends, and they made you feel worthless. Then Brock came along, and you're on top of the world."

They talked about the bullying and Matthew brought up the bullying from his church.

"How did the church make you feel?"

Matthew told Rich about the messages from the pulpit and how he had no one to talk about it with. He explained how he rejected the church because of how they treated him.

"Would you say you carry those negative views with you still?"

"Sometimes when I'm feeling low. There are so many people who feel justified to put gays down, and spew negative things. When I'm strong, I can dismiss the statements but not always. If I had someone love me for who I am I would be able to cope. I felt that way when I was with Brock."

"Our time is up for today and I think we're getting somewhere. You may not feel like we are, but today, we went down that next layer I talked about. Next week we'll continue."

"See you then."

Making A Difference

Chapter 18

It was difficult to concentrate on anything with the expansion underway. Tom came into Mackenzie's office, "Holding a therapy session without interruption has become my newest challenge. The construction noises are intrusive. I go to the farthest end, and I get a bit of respite, but it's always there. I've taken to having the resident go with me for a walk and that, although not ideal, helps us get away from the noise. How are you managing?"

"I'm getting a whole lot better ignoring things and wearing this noise-cancelling headset helps a lot. The only inconvenience is I have to watch for the light on the phone when it rings. The good thing is that it won't be for a long time."

It was mid-morning, and the residents were coming and going. Everyone was doing their best to cope. Emily walked by with Joanne, another resident, and waved to Tom and Mackenzie. Tom returned a small wave and then asked, "What will you two be doing to deal with the expansion noise?"

A blast from a jack hammer punctuated Tom's question and Emily rolled her eyes, "We're going for a long walk. Let's get our coats and then we'll head out." They turned and walked up the stairs.

Tom and Mackenzie continued to talk when a woman in her forties walked in. Tom was the first person she saw and went over to him, "I'm hoping you can help me. My name is Mollie Fraser, and I'm looking for Callie, our daughter. She has been missing for several weeks and nothing we've done has helped find her. I had called all the shelters and her friends when she first went missing but no one admitted she was anywhere. The other day, I had a thought that maybe she wasn't using her name. I hope she's still in the area so I thought I'd check in person. Here is a picture of my daughter. Is she here?"

Joanne was the first down the stairs, so she waited. Emily saw her waiting and yelled to her, "How did you get out so fast?"

Mollie heard the voice and spun around before Tom or Mackenzie could look at the picture, "Callie!"

Emily stopped and looked at her mother, "What are you doing here?"

"Oh, Callie, I'm so glad I found you!" She ran forward but Emily backed away. "Your dad and I've been worried sick about you."

Making A Difference

"You should have thought about that before you kicked me out. You didn't seem too worried when I left."

Molly knew she was in front of strangers so she composed herself so she wouldn't react and say something she would regret later, "We weren't thinking and reacted before we had our wits about us. We want you to come home."

"And what are the conditions on me living in your home? You walked in on me with my girlfriend and freaked. I'm lesbian. Can you support me living openly or would you want me to hide who I really am?"

Molly was horrified that Callie spoke so openly, "I've been to a Pflag meeting and your father and I are reading books which the leaders gave me. I'm learning a lot so if you're patient with me, I think we'll come to accept your lifestyle."

"Mom, it isn't a lifestyle. Vegan is a lifestyle, being a recycler is a lifestyle, being religious is a lifestyle. Those are all things I can choose. I am lesbian, something I did not choose. I was born this way and the only choice I can make is to hide it or live my life in truth to who I am. I've stopped hiding and making up a life you can accept. This is me." She paused, "Except here I'm Emily because I didn't want you to find me."

Mackenzie had gone into the hall in case Emily needed some support, but she was proud she wasn't being subservient to her mother.

Molly handled the information with composure, "If we say we'll allow you to be lesbian, will you come home with me?"

"Allow me! Mom, you haven't heard me. You don't have a say in me being a lesbian. There is no allowing. So, you're going to Pflag meetings. I know several friends who have benefited from attending. How about I meet you halfway."

Molly asked, "What does that mean?"

"It means that I'll start being in your lives while I live here. We attend Pflag meetings together so you learn about what having a lesbian daughter means, and only when you accept me and any partner I have in my life, will I agree to move back home."

Molly looked to Mackenzie and Tom for support. "Help me here."

Tom spoke first, "I've been talking with Emily or Callie and she knows what she wants. She has given you a fair compromise and I applaud her sound reasoning. No one wants to live a life that isn't true to who they are."

Mackenzie joined in, "The Pflag leaders are my parents, Martha and Grant Matheson and they went through a very difficult time when my brother came out. I

Making A Difference

think Pflag is exactly what your family needs right now. I suggest you and your husband take her up on her offer if you want her back in your lives."

Molly didn't look thrilled, "Alright Callie, we'll go to Pflag meetings, the next one is this Friday at 7pm. Do you want us to pick you up?"

"That'll be great. I want you and Dad to feel welcome here for visits as long as you accept and respect me. If you cross the line, you'll have to leave."

Molly nodded, "I think we can do that. Is there a number I can call to let you know I'm coming over?"

Mackenzie scooted into her office and returned with a business card, "Call this number and I'll make sure I give her the message." She looked at Emily, "Is it OK with you to change our records from Emily to Callie Fraser?"

Callie smiled, "I guess I'm not hiding anymore so yes; you can change your records."

*****

The Pflag meeting was running well with lots of conversation while Callie and her parents, Molly and Jim Fraser sat quietly watching and listening. The topic being discussed was *'coming out'* and Callie thought her parents might participate but they just sat there.

Callie listened and a lady across the room was talking about her son coming out to her. She summed up her thoughts and Callie decided to jump in, "As I explained in the introductions, this is Mom and Dad. I didn't exactly come out to them in any organized fashion." She explained her mom walking in on her making out with her girlfriend, asking the girlfriend to leave, and calling her dad home and the whole ugly scene that followed. "When they kicked me out of my home, I left and changed my name so they couldn't find me. We've agreed to come to these meetings so we can become a family again. I'll not move home until they accept me for who I am and respect me by welcoming my girlfriend when she visits me."

Molly felt compelled to speak, "Jim and I do not understand why she thinks she's a lesbian, but we're opening ourselves up to learn. Martha and Grant loaned me a few books which we're reading, and we're learning things we never thought about before. At least Callie has allowed us to visit her at the homeless shelter. I think our first visit went well; wouldn't you say Jim?"

Jim looked startled and now he felt pressure. "It was good to see Callie again and I'm glad she's giving us time to sort this out. Personally, I never knew any gay or lesbian people and was taught it was abnormal. I'm having a difficult time figuring all of this out, but I'm hoping the books help."

Martha spoke, "Jim, we were never taught about LGBT so, of course, it's a shock. What we need to do is educate ourselves. There are support group meetings, websites, books, and people to talk to and all or any of those resources will help us grow in our understanding. The most important thing to keep in mind is to not let any misinformed bigots make you feel you need to reject your child. Open yourself to learning and love your daughter. Things will start to fit together."

Grant smiled, "Jim, I applaud you for coming to the meeting. When my son came out, I kicked him out because I thought he chose being gay or was influenced by other gay people and I wanted him to choose not to be gay. I now know I was very ignorant about the LGBT world. Martha and my daughter, Mackenzie pushed me hard, and after refusing to attend several meetings, Martha used some force, so I finally attended but under duress. It was an uphill battle, but I finally let go of my old views and learned about my son's life. We're a family again and nothing beats family."

*****

It was the end of the day and Tom stood at Mackenzie's door waiting for her to end her phone call. She was jotting down notes and hadn't noticed he was there until she reached for a highlighter, and something caught her attention. She pointed to the phone and held up two fingers. He waited.

She ended her call, "So, Tom, what can I do for you?"

He was nervous but composed himself, "You can say you'll go out on a date with me."

Makenzie looked surprised, "I'd love to go out with you, Tom. You said date, did you mean it?"

A smile swept across his face removing all hints of any nervousness, "Yes, I meant I want us to start dating. Since I met you, I've been impressed with who you are as a person, and you offer something none of my other girlfriends have. I admire your values and ethics, I love your compassion and empathy for others, and all I've been thinking about since our last dinner is I want more of you in my life. Can we try being a couple?"

"Thank you, Tom. I feel the same about you. I'd like to try being a couple. What would you like to do for our first date?"

Making A Difference

"I have a surprise planned. You'll need to change into more casual jeans and a top so I'll pick you up at six."

Mackenzie giggled about the response she was about to give, "It's a date. See you at six."

*****

Tom showed up ten minutes early as Mackenzie expected and went out to the car in a flash, "You do have a thing about being early. It's a good thing I know you."

"I don't know why I persist in being early, everyone else makes me wait. You don't, that's one more thing I like about you!"

"Are you going to tell me where we're going?"

"No, I want you to find out when we arrive."

They drove off and Mackenzie was analysing the route and trying to determine what might be at the end of this drive. She failed. He slowed and turned into a church parking lot.

A puzzled Mackenzie queried, "We're going to church?"

Tom laughed, "Not quite. We're going to the church hall." He parked and went into the trunk while Mackenzie got out of the car and stood looking at all the other parked cars. "Come over here." She went to the back of the car and Tom held up cowboy hats and boots. "We're going to a hoedown! There is a buffet and square dancing! I had to sneak into your office to find out your shoe size." He sat on the car bumper to put on his boots.

Mackenzie put on the hat and boots, and responded, "They fit perfectly. Yee haw, this will be fun."

Tom crooked his arm, "I saw this advertised and decided we needed a fun first date." He switched into a country drawl, "Come with me, darlin."

She looped her arm through his and off they went.

Making A Difference

Chapter 19

Gregory suggested that Neal arrive early so he could meet all of the guys as they arrived. He was introduced to Andrew, and they talked about safe topics because Andrew knew he would be nervous.

Neal offered to help set up for dinner, "If I have something to concentrate on, it'll keep me from becoming so nervous and be sick to my stomach." He got the dishes out and set the table complete with cutlery, stemware, and napkins.

Gregory was admiring his precision, "Where did you learn how to set such an exact table?"

"I worked at the Trade and Convention Centre, and we had many very formal events. Sam, the head waiter, was OCD, at least we believed he was. He had a ruler in his back pocket while the tables were being set and would measure the placement of everything. I guess after screwing up once too many times, I began to place everything, so he was never able to admonish me. I took great satisfaction in knowing things were perfect."

Andrew and Gregory went over the names and a summary of each of the seven guys who were coming. They told him who had dated whom, and who were still together as well as who was single. They had just finished when they heard a car drive in.

Brock and Dirk gave a quick knock and went inside. Introductions were made all around and Andrew asked questions of Dirk to become more acquainted with him. As he was winding down, another car drove in. Jeremy and Henry were welcomed in and went through introductions.

Neal remembered something and spoke to Henry, "Are you and Jeremy a couple?"

Henry was a bit surprised but answered, "We used to be, in high school but now we're just good friends.

Another car drove in with Anson, Matthew, and Charles. They were welcomed and introduced to Neal and Dirk. Brock watched Matthew's face go rigid when Andrew introduced Dirk as his boyfriend. He regretted not preparing Matthew for that news. In no time, all ten guys were chatting and getting to know one another. Gregory brought out appetizers and Andrew poured drinks for

Making A Difference

everyone. As the appetizers disappeared Andrew and Gregory moved into preparing to serve the main course.

Gregory announced, "OK guys, if everyone would take a seat, we can continue our chatter during supper."

Neal and Dirk were getting to know the others and Andrew noticed that Matthew, Jeremy, and Henry were paying particular attention to Neal. The conversation was interesting, and everyone learned new things about their old and new friends. After dessert was finished, Andrew suggested they move into the living room and play a game to get to know each other better.

He introduced the game as a series of rounds where each of the guys would answer questions about themselves on several topics. By the end of the game everyone had learned a lot about each other. There were moments when laughter broke out and teasing ensued when something suggestive came out like Dirk being able to touch his tongue to the tip of his nose.

During the game, Neal told them he played the guitar and wrote songs so when the game was over, Matthew told him he would like to hear him play sometime. The rest of the guys joined in and suggested he bring his guitar to their next get together.

Neal responded, "I have my guitar in the car, would you like to do a sing-along?" They encouraged him to get the guitar and before long, he was playing and singing. The shyness was gone, and he transformed into the life of the party. He played songs everyone knew and encouraged them to sing with him.

Gregory was pleased to see the room come alive with music and watched as one by one the guys joined in. The night had gone well and even though he and Andrew were old enough to be the grandfathers for the room full of young men, it felt like they belonged. He knew the guys would include Neal in their lives and he suspected that one of the single guys would be vying to have him as their boyfriend. He smiled and thought, *'Life is good!'*

*****

Andrew motioned to Brock to follow him into the office area. The rest of the guys were in lively conversation so they knew they could take a few minutes.

Andrew explained Stan and Oliver's dilemma with his sick mother and homophobic brother and not being able to afford to visit her. He summarized their situation, "We would give them the money but with holding the mortgage for Kaleisha, we're strapped. Do you think they would qualify for some money from your charity?"

Making A Difference

Brock nodded, "Yes, especially where the homophobia is causing them to spend money they shouldn't have to. How much do you think they'll need?"

"I've given this much thought and for a two-week stay, I think it will cost them over ten thousand for them both to go."

"I've got some cheques in my bag." He retrieved the bag and returned to the office. "I'll make this out for Twelve thousand. If they need more, let me know."

"Thank you, Brock. It does my heart good to be able to help Oliver see his mother."

*****

It was after midnight when Brock announced he had to get up early in the morning and got ready to leave. He looked out to the parking area, "Jeremy, is your car parked behind mine?"

"Yes." He looked at Henry, "We might as well go too."

The four of them said goodbyes all round and exchanged contact information with Neal. Anson and Charles were ready to go as well but Matthew seemed to want to stay longer.

Neal noticed Matthew's hesitation and suggested, "I can drive you home if you don't want to leave just yet. You said you lived uptown, and I live on the west side so I can drop you on my way by."

Matthew was thrilled, "That would be great Neal, thank you!" He looked to Anson and Charles, "Thanks for the lift out. I'll go back with Neal."

Anson winked at Matthew, "See you at the office tomorrow." He looked at Andrew and Gregory, "Thank you for the wonderful supper and delightful evening." He turned to Neal, "It was nice meeting you and now that we have your contact information, we'll keep in touch. See you later." Charles nodded along with what Anson said and waved as they left.

After waving from the door, Andrew and Gregory came back into the living space and noticed Matthew and Neal were deep in conversation, so they cleaned up the kitchen. When they were done, they sat across from Neal and Matthew. "So, Neal, did tonight work out well for you?"

Neal grinned, "This was great! I now have people I can connect with and someone to talk things over with. I don't feel alone. It's getting late so we should leave. Is that OK Matthew?"

"Yes, I'm ready."

Making A Difference

The moment wasn't lost on Andrew and Gregory. Ten minutes ago, Matthew didn't want to leave with Anson and Charles. They knew he wanted to leave with Neal.

They waved goodbye as they backed out of the driveway.

*****

The next morning Andrew called Stan and Oliver and invited them to breakfast. They arrived and Oliver said, "This is a nice, spontaneous surprise! Whatever we're having will go better with mimosas!" He held up the champagne and orange juice. "We just happened to have some in the fridge after a little thing we did last week. One of our guests brought it and left the remainder. How great is that!"

Gregory was ready to start, "That will work well. We're having poached eggs on toast with bacon and fruit on the side."

The table was set, Gregory was poaching the eggs, Stan was putting some fruit on each plate, and Andrew managed the toast. Soon they were eating and chatting.

Andrew put an envelope on the table in front of Oliver. "This is for both of you."

Oliver looked puzzled, "What's this? Doesn't matter, it's for us and I can't wait any longer!" He tore the envelope open and read the note out loud:

'Oliver and Stan,

Since the other night when you told us about your mom and the obnoxious brother, we reached out to a philanthropist and got this money so you both can go visit without being beholden to your brother.

Love,

Gregory & Andrew'

Oliver looked at the cheque and burst into tears. He sat there crying and shaking and Stan wasn't far behind. Once they composed themselves, they gave each of the guys tight, prolonged hugs, "You guys! You're something else. Thank you!"

Gregory slapped Stan on the back, "So, you need to deposit that cheque and start booking your trip!"

*****

Making A Difference

Matthew walked into the office with more energy than he has had for a while. He greeted Anson, "Good morning, Anson. Wasn't that a great night out with the guys?"

"It was. The food was great, the conversation flowed well, and we got to know more about each other. How well did you get to know Neal?"

Matthew smiled, "Neal is a great guy and so new to the gay world. We talked on the way home and he appreciated that the guys set up the evening for him. He knows no gay people other than the group at the party. It's been years since I came out, I can barely remember what it was like."

"Some things you don't forget but we must admit the world is changing and only when I meet someone like Neal, I forget it hasn't changed enough. His parents are super religious, so you're the one to help him in that department."

"My God, he's handsome, and so talented. He sings like an angel and plays the guitar so well. I think I'm in love. Lust for sure but maybe more than that. Time will tell."

"Man, you're in over your head, 'He sings like an angel.', that line comes right out of a Hallmark romance. Did you make plans to get together again?"

Matthew shrugged, "We're connecting tomorrow somewhere. Since we both still live with our parents, there isn't a place we can go where we can be comfortable. I did show him the Fort Howe lookout and we parked for about half an hour, but he got so spooked by the other traffic, we hardly kissed."

Anson's face lit up with surprise, "You kissed?"

"Yes, we were talking, and he leaned over and gave me an awkward peck. I took his head in my hands and gave him a real kiss. It was his first ever. He had never even kissed a girl."

"Are you going to come back to earth and get some work done today?"

"Oh, I'll get work done but I'll be smiling all day! I have a good concept of what Brock wants for phase two. I need to hire a survey company to tell me where the lake is in relation to the property lines. Once I have, I can place things in the design where I need them to be to create the effect Brock spoke about. I'm so pleased he came to me so I could do it."

"How were you with Brock having that hunk, Dirk, as a boyfriend? I saw your face react when he was introduced. You weren't expecting that."

"I was dumbfounded. When he came to me earlier this week, I fantasized he wanted us to get back together, and this design was the excuse he needed to get in touch. I don't know how I couldn't have reacted because it was like getting

Making A Difference

punched in the gut. If I could hide that, I need to get myself to Hollywood because that would have been Oscar worthy."

"You seemed to recover quickly once Neal was introduced."

Matthew opened up, "I must admit, Neal was a great distraction. I have to say he took my attention so well, I paid little attention to Dirk and Brock. I do have to admit they do make a handsome couple."

"That they do. Now, go get the land surveyors hired!"

Making A Difference

Chapter 20

Brock arrived for Sunday supper and found Mackenzie in the kitchen talking with their parents, "Sorry I'm late, but I got tied up with Pine Valley work. What did I miss?"

"I was just telling Mom & Dad about how the shelter is weathering the expansion. So far so good, but there will be issues when they break through the roof to connect the floors with the staircase. I'm not concerning myself now, but we'll deal with that when we have to. What's new with you Bro?"

"I've met a wonderful man and we've been on three or four dates. His name is Dirk, he's an IT developer who made a lot of money selling an app. He owns his own virtual IT development company which he runs out of his home."

Martha was pleased to hear Brock's news but wanted to know, "How did you meet Dirk?"

Brock explained the chance meeting at the garden centre, how he delivered and helped plant the tree, and about being invited for supper. He left out any intimate details but included most of the rest in the explanation. He talked about hiring Matthew to do the second phase of Pine Valley and got excited as he spoke about the pavilion with the view of the lake and the botanical gardens.

Mackenzie furrowed her brow, "You're talking to Matthew? He hasn't contacted me since he broke things off with you and I haven't pursued any friendship with him. If I met him on the street, I'd greet him but so much time has gone by I believe he didn't want to be friends with me."

"Since he did the first design, I wanted him to finish it. I didn't have the land at that time but now that we know what the site offers, I want him to use the area and design the buildings for the best use of the property. So, I put my pettiness aside and went to see him at their office. I'm glad I did, and we even spoke about becoming friends again."

Grant listened and commented, "I've seen him around and had a few conversations, but he's always very guarded."

Martha spoke up, "Supper is ready so let's continue this conversation at the table."

Things were quiet as they dished out their food and only started talking once Grant said grace.

Making A Difference

Martha picked up where they left off in the kitchen, "So, you'll be friends. How do you think it will look now that Dirk is in the picture? Does Matthew know about him?"

"Well, Andrew and Gregory had a gathering to introduce a not-out gay man to some gay people and they asked me if I minded Matthew being invited. I had no problem but when he arrived and I introduced Dirk, his face told me he was more than surprised. I felt bad but then he was introduced to Neal, and he seemed to soften the blow. I didn't realize how awkward it would be but that lasted only minutes before Matthew's attention was diverted. All in all, it was more comfortable than I expected." Brock took a roll and buttered it.

Martha joined in, "I'm so glad you and Matthew will be friends. I like him. Over time, maybe he could visit for supper. So, Mackenzie, Brock has Dirk, and you were saying Tom could be boyfriend material. Anything happening there?"

Mackenzie looked at her mother with alarm, "Mom! That was kind of direct. Well, we continue to talk, and we've been out a couple of times as friends but that's my call. I believe Tom wants to be more than friends. I just need to wrap my head around what having my boyfriend as an employee looks like and how I manage the dynamics."

Martha offered, "The thing you have going for you is that the shelter has few employees and the ones you have, all do different jobs. The way I see it, if you had two therapists, there might be a point where one might become jealous of how Tom is treated and accuse you of favouritism even if there isn't any. That's just the way jealousy in the workplace unfolds. In my job as Dean of Science, I've seen this happen many times in a year, but I think small is good. If you feel Tom is boyfriend material, set some clear ground rules about relationship and work and then jump in."

"I appreciate your words of wisdom."

Grant felt it was time to get away from where the conversation had taken them, "We have work to do on the information Father Mike bequeathed me. We finally have it all sorted, and we've done a bit of analysis, where do we go from here?"

Martha jumped right in, "I want to reiterate that I'm concerned about the damage that will be caused by opening old wounds. I don't care about the Church, but I do care about the victims of abuse."

Mackenzie nodded, "I'm in complete agreement Mom. I don't want the Church to get away with their hiding the abuse, so we need to find a way to protect the victims while taking the Church to task. I wonder if this is too big for the four of us and if we could let someone else do the dirty work." She checked to see that her parents weren't looking and winked at Brock.

Brock caught the wink and opened with, "I watched a show about abuse and journalists took the material, did some investigation and wrote a front-page story. It blew up bigger than they expected and many abuse victims came forward. Finally, someone would listen to them. Could we look at giving this information to a journalist or maybe a lawyer?"

Grant was thoughtful, "Journalists would need their editors to OK their work but if they didn't, the information dies. Giving it to a lawyer would be expensive."

Brock looked at Mackenzie and she nodded, "Dad, Mammie left me a lot of money that I could use to fund this. If the lawyer wins, they could get their costs back from the church."

Grant looked at Brock, "Son, she left you with a nest egg that you might need if you're doing phase two so I'd be concerned you would lose it all."

"Mom, Dad, I haven't spoken about what she left me except to three people. Mackenzie, Andrew, and Gregory were available when you didn't want me in the family and getting word of the size of the inheritance shocked me. I had to talk to someone and those three know but I made them promise they would not tell anyone. Mammie was able to live with her fortune without people knowing and I want to do the same. I have lots of money."

Martha teared up, "I so regret what we did to you when we kicked you out, but I'm glad you had the guys and your sister to talk to. You said fortune, what kind of fortune?"

Brock looked to Mackenzie and shrugged, "Please don't tell anyone because I'm concerned about someone kidnapping of all three of you and any future generations. I haven't looked at the amount in a while but there has to be more than one hundred million." He let that sit in the air.

Grant looked at Brock and then at Martha, "One hundred million dollars!"

Brock nodded, "Yes. I don't see how I could possibly spend it all in fifty lifetimes. Mackenzie and I formed a philanthropic foundation, which built the shelter and is now expanding it, helped homeless people get university degrees, helped people in need, paid for medical procedures or drugs when the people couldn't afford them, and whatever came across our desk when people needed money. Aside from the foundation, I'm using some of my own money to build phase two at Pine Valley. I have to be careful, so people won't know I'm rich."

Making A Difference

Martha whistled, "Wow, my son is a millionaire! As much as I want to yell this from the rooftops, I understand your concern about security and the evil forces out there who could target our family. Alice was one smart lady!"

Grant agreed, "That she was! You have my word that this information doesn't go any further. So, back to what we do. How do we decide?"

Mackenzie offered, "Let's take a step back and analyse what outcome we want to achieve. As I see it, everyone knows about the abuse from the Church. When I did the research for you, Dad, there were many stories about the abuse so if a journalist writes a story, so what?"

Grant thought about Mackenzie's question, "You're right; so what? If we're going to make a difference it would be for the abuse victims. Maybe a story would be the start of it so the victims would come forward with the promise of a class-action lawsuit against the Church."

Mackenzie agreed, "Let's try looking for a journalist who might want to write the story. This could make the career of any ambitious person."

Brock spoke up, "I've thought about the opportunity we're potentially offering to someone. We could have a seasoned journalist or a very ambitious young one, but I'm leaning toward a seasoned one. We could present the option to a few journalists and see if anyone wants to do this. Maybe we should have the lawyer on board to help us determine what we need to do."

"I'll begin researching journalists and looking into which lawyers would do a case like this." Mackenzie offered.

Grant suggested, "One thing I know is, we'll have to give them the documents so, I think we should make copies."

Brock agreed, "That's a good idea. I'll take the boxes and make four sets. We'll pass out the copies but keep the originals."

Making A Difference

Chapter 21

Mackenzie blocked out the world reviewing the monthly budget in her office and didn't notice the two visitors who came in. She came back to reality when she heard Molly and Jim knock on her door. "Good morning, Jim and Molly, how are you doing today?"

Molly stepped into the office, "We're doing well. The Pflag meetings and the resource material your parents lent us is helping us understand what Callie's world is like. I think we're making progress, but it's hard not to fall back to the old life we had planned for her."

Mackenzie nodded, "Besides being concerned for the health and well-being of their child, most parents have to mourn the life they sculpted out for their loved ones. Then they realize their child can still have a very similar life just that their partner would be of the same gender. Are you here to see Callie?"

"Yes, but we wanted to talk to you first. We told Callie we'd meet here at 11 o'clock so that gives us half an hour if you have the time."

Mackenzie looked down at the papers on her desk and asked herself what was more important, "This budget stuff was getting to me so let's go find a conversation area and have a chat." She left her office, and they went to the far end of living space. After they were seated, Mackenzie asked, "So, what would you like to talk about?"

Jim spoke for the first time, "We want Callie to come home, but she doesn't trust we're ready. Is there a way she could keep her room for a week and try living home so if it doesn't work out, she has a place to come?"

There was a loud boom and Mackenzie startled. "I just need to make sure everything is OK. I'll be back soon." She scooted off toward where the boom came from.

Molly looked at Jim, "I hope there's a way to do this so there can be a transition for Callie."

Jim started wringing his hands, "I know we want her home but what if we mess up and she ends up hating us?"

"Remember, our only job is to love her. If we can keep to that, we should be able to keep mess-ups to a minimum. It must have been ok because here comes Mackenzie."

Mackenzie sat down, "It was just part of the expansion work; nothing to be concerned about." She got back to their question and summarized what she thought they had asked her.

Making A Difference

"Yes, we want a buffer for Callie."

"Here's what I can do. I'll keep her room available for one week, after that I have to allow it to be given to someone looking for a place. Does Callie know you're asking her to move home?"

"Not yet. We wanted to check with you first and then when we see her, we can ask her."

Mackenzie looked at the time, "She should be coming down shortly, do you want me to be part of the discussion?"

Jim shrugged his shoulders, "There are no instructions for this kind of thing, so we're not sure what the right thing to do is. I think I'd like us to propose her coming home and explain your offer for a week. If she has any questions we can't answer, can we call on you then?"

"Sure, I'll just be in my office working on the budget, so I'd probably enjoy the distraction." She stood to go, "Bye for now."

She had just gotten into her office when Callie appeared looking around for her parents. Jim and Molly stood and waved to catch her eye. Callie spotted them and walked over. She gave each a hug and sat down. They explained their proposal and Mackenzie's offer.

Callie sat listening and her parents could see she was weighing things over in her mind. Jim couldn't wait any longer, "What do you think?"

Callie opened up, "I'd love to move home but only if it's welcoming and not critical or judgmental of me and my life. Mom, Dad, you have to accept I am lesbian, and I want to be able to have my girlfriend welcomed just like you would welcome a boyfriend if I had one. The minute I don't feel accepted, and respected, I am out."

Molly sat up, "This is all new to us and we aren't going to be perfect parents; we never were before so how can you expect us to be now. I don't want to be walking on eggshells in my home so can we add something. Instead of you getting mad and leaving, you need to let us know we messed up and give us the opportunity to correct our behaviours. Can this work?"

Callie thought about the request, "I think that's fair but let's start off on the right foot and create ground rules, so we have the same expectations."

Jim looked between Molly and Callie, "What kind of ground rules? At work we have ground rules that help us manage our meetings, are you suggesting something like those?"

Callie suggested, "Yes, you'll probably see similar ones, but you'll also see different ones because of the situation. Maybe we could develop them here. There's

Making A Difference

a room with a white board where we can brainstorm. I'd like to ask Tom if he'd help. Is this OK?"

Molly jumped up, "Sure is. Lead the way to the room. We can ask Tom when we go by his office."

They put their things in the room while Callie went to Tom's office and asked him. He agreed and followed her to the room. He agreed to facilitate the brainstorming.

Tom pointed out the meeting ground rules posted on the wall, "We'll follow those to allow us to brainstorm your ground rules. Everyone agree?"

Callie remarked, "I do. They're all about respecting each other in one way or another. If we can follow those, we can get this done quickly."

Jim read the list to himself, "These are very similar to the ones we have at work. I agree with them."

Molly smiled, "I agree as well. Let's hope getting our ground rules written will be as easy."

Tom announced, "It will be very important that we really hear what's being said. I'll record everything you come up with. Once we've exhausted all ideas, we'll go through a process of understanding what each means and combining like ideas. In the end we'll land on your ground rules."

For the next hour, Tom used his process to end up with eight ground rules everyone agreed with, "I want each of you to think about this list and ask yourself if you can abide by these."

Callie got a sense from the conversations during the brainstorming that her parents wanted her home and were ready to make her feel comfortable. She looked at her parents, "If you can live with these ground rules and I get to call you out when you violate them, I think we can live together. Let's give it a week and see how it works out."

They thanked Tom who looked very pleased with the work they accomplished. Callie went over to Mackenzie's office, knocked, and walked in. She explained what they had done and about her decision. She thanked her for the one week as a back up and told her she would be taking some of her things but not all. If the week worked out with her parents, she would clear out of her room at the end of the week. "Thank you for making a difference in my life. I appreciate all that you, Tom, and this shelter does and hope you'll soon have my room to share with another person who needs it."

"You're always welcome here. I wish you the best." She got up from her desk and hugged Callie tightly. "Stay in touch, I'll miss you!"

Making A Difference

Callie got her things and left with her parents.

*****

Callie felt a little weird entering her home. She had a blast of memory of the day her parents kicked her out and she shook her head to rid herself of the emotional pain which accompanied that particular memory.

Molly put her things on the closest chair, "I'm going to heat up some chicken corn chowder from yesterday. Callie, you put your things in your bedroom and come down for lunch. Jim, we'll be eating in fifteen minutes." Everyone scattered in different directions.

Callie plugged the charger into the phone and called Emma, her girlfriend. "I've moved home to see how things will work out. I want you to come visit tomorrow to see if my parents will accept you as my girlfriend."

Emma was surprised, "Wow, that's a big step! Do you think they'll be able to accept you and your new world?"

"They say they can." She explained the ground rules to Emma, "I have great hope. I said I'd try this for a week and determine what happens then."

When they finished talking, Callie said, "I have to go down for lunch. Let's plan your visit for 1 o'clock. We can kick around here for a couple of hours and then go out somewhere. That should give them a good taste of my life."

*****

The week flew by, and Callie put her parents through every test she could dream up. A few times, they had to use their ground rules for something wasn't working out but when calmer heads prevailed things worked out to her satisfaction. By the end of the week, they got together and reviewed how the week went. Callie told them if they could behave the way they did that week through all of her tests, she could live there. She went to inform Mackenzie and Tom at the shelter of her decision, reviewed the week and its challenges, packed up her room, and turned in her keys. They hugged and she walked away.

Mackenzie yelled after her, "Don't be a stranger!"

Tom walked over and stood beside Mackenzie as she watched Callie leave, "Does it bother you when someone you got to know moves out?"

"No, I'm happy for them that they got their life back. With Callie, her parents worked hard to understand her and are making great progress in making her feel she's back in a family that loves here. I celebrate the successes."

Making A Difference

*****

Mackenzie sat with a smile reflecting on the fun they had at the hoedown and how it was a wonderful start to their coupledom. They had so much fun together stumbling through the square dance steps and bumping into people when they went one way instead of the other. The people were welcoming, the food was great, and the evening was filled with laughter. They had their first kiss at the end of the third dance. When Tom drove Mackenzie home, she invited him in, and they snuggled on the couch talking about things they liked and were thrilled that they had so much in common.

Talk gave way to some heavy kissing and Tom had become aroused. They talked about where they needed to go but he stopped any further discussion, "As much as I want to go with you to your bedroom, I don't want our first date to end that way. Now, our second date, that's a whole different story!"

They both agreed and laughed about how traditional the whole waiting thing sounded. Mackenzie said, "I can't wait for our second date."

Tom responded, "Me too."

Chapter 22

Carson enjoyed the ride to the cottage and relaxed into the country feel. When he walked up to the door, he could see Andrew and Gregory sitting at the island in the kitchen. He gave a little knock before walking in. "Good morning, guys, are you ready for me?"

"I think we are. We have that tea you like already for you, and I made some cinnamon rolls." Andrew said as he brought the items to the coffee table.

Carson took a cinnamon roll, "These are still warm, did you just bake them?"

Andrew smiled, "Just for your visit."

Carson took a drink, smacked his lips and announced, "This is amazing, I'm moving in!"

Both guys nodded to each other, and Gregory offered, "We have a spare room so if that will help the book, we would be open to having you live here for a bit. Let's put some dates in our calendars."

Carson closed his calendar. "This will help me get the book done quicker, thanks. So, let's get to work. Last interview, you gave me a lot of activities and I'd like more detail on each. Let's take them one at a time. About the Human Rights complaint you lodged against Elaine Payne, your Member of Parliament, when was it evident to you that your MP wasn't an ally in your fight for equality?"

Andrew started, "I guess it started when she was the city's mayor. When we bought the building that is now Mahogany Manor, Elaine showed up at our door one night with her assistant. She was friendly and asked what we were doing and seemed interested in the idea we were going to open a Bed and Breakfast. The visit left us with a good feeling. A short time after the visit, a friend of ours who worked in the city's Tourism Department told us that a group of travel writers were going to visit Saint John. As part of the planning, someone had suggested that each Bed and Breakfast in the city offer a free night's stay for one of the travel writers. He told us Elaine had been in on one of the meetings and said, "I have friends who are opening a B&B on Germain Street. Do not place any of the travel writers in their B&B because they're gay, and we wouldn't want any negative situations to come up. That was our first inkling she was a bigot. A funny aside to this story is that we didn't open the B&B until 1994 so they couldn't have stayed there anyway but the whole group of travel writers were doing a tour. Two of the earlier people saw the house and asked if they could see the inside. They loved it and were excited to show the rest so every one of the travel writers ended up in our home that day. I think Elaine would have had a stroke if she had known."

Gregory continued, "When she became our MP in the early 2000s when LGBT equality surfaced in Parliament, she was an outspoken opponent to the gay community. One day we wanted to speak with her and try to get her to understand, she denied us access and refused to meet with a group of gays. That same day, she appeared in King's Square and spoke at a Christian rally against same-gender marriage. Part of her speech was inviting the group to meet with her, that she had an open door for them and would be glad to discuss the issue. She afforded the Christian Right an open door and slammed it in the LGBT community's face. That was what caused us to launch a complaint based on discrimination because we're gay. We felt she needed to represent all of her constituents."

Carson was interested, "What was the outcome to that complaint?"

"The ruling came out that, as an elected representative, she had no requirement to meet with anyone. They said our complaint needed to be handled at the polls. The problem with that thinking is that marginalized groups do not get polls to be in their favour as long as the bigots are a majority. To us it was a lame outcome, but we had other areas that needed our attention, so we dropped it."

Carson needed to know, "Were there other issues with Elaine?"

Andrew thought, "Well, she was very vocal in Parliament and one day she got up and said several bigoted statements about gay men. She was an embarrassment to our city and most of the gay community couldn't believe her being so open about her bigotry. Because of her words, we organized the first Pride parade in Saint John. That was 2003 and we can thank her for her bigotry because that's the one thing that mobilized the gay community when nothing else did. In a roundabout way, we give her the credit and she actually won an award from the gay community for what she did. I'm sure she never kept the award; she probably destroyed it the minute she opened it, but we don't know that for sure. We always had hoped she would become enlightened, but I don't believe that ever happened."

Carson finished his sentence and punctuated it with a distinct tap of the pen, "I think that's all for today." He looked at his calendar, "So I'll be back in two days, and we can work almost a full three days into the early evening on Saturday. I'll pack a bag and be out here by 8:00 for breakfast as we agreed. The more you tell me, the more I'm looking forward to our conversations. I do have to admit though, I'm really looking forward to your scrumptious meals almost as much, if not more!"

Everyone laughed. Andrew and Gregory walked with Carson to the door, chatted a bit and bid him goodbye.

Making A Difference

*****

When Carson arrived on Thursday, breakfast was almost ready, "Good morning, guys! Whatever you're cooking smells fantastic; is there anything I can help with?"

Gregory had the oven door down and was testing something with a skewer, "I made a frittata, and it will be done in about five minutes, "You can start the toast if you want."

Andrew was setting the table, so Carson went to work making the toast, "Did you make this bread?"

Andrew smiled, "Yes, we love toast made out of home-made bread."

Carson rolled his eyes, "Of course you do! I suppose you have an assortment of jams and jellies you made as well."

Andrew nodded, "Yes, we made them all. Would you prefer we buy jam for you?"

"I'll suffer through wonderfully home-made foods. You know, if you keep this up, I may never leave." Carson chuckled at his wit.

The guys joined in with Carson's chuckle and the good humour lasted through breakfast and into the interview.

"So, let's keep working on the other activities you were involved in." Carson said as he positioned his pen to write.

Gregory and Andrew spoke at once but brought out different situations.

Carson stopped them by placing his palm in the air. "OK, Gregory, what were you sharing? Andrew, I'll get to you next."

Gregory recalled what he had said, "I was thinking about us being refused putting a float in the Christmas parade. There were several people who worked together to make things better in small ways. We had decided that if the community could see involvement from the LGBT community in regular events, it would do a couple of things; we would be visible and the people would see we weren't scary, LGBT people would see themselves in regular events, and our message would be getting out. The cure for the ignorance we would regularly hear is education and in little ways, we decided to educate others. Our goal was to place a float in the city's annual Christmas parade to show an LGBT Christmas which wouldn't be much different than the non-LGBT community except for the use of the Pride colours in our decorations. A simple gesture which was thwarted when Barbara Macauley, the mayor at the time, refused to allow us in because, in her words *'the Christmas parade was no place for sex'*. We were refused because the mayor had a stereotype that we would somehow depict sex on our float. This was blatant prejudice based on her belief of the gay community, so Andrew met with Barbara to try to educate her and defend our proposal. She listened but, in the end, said her decision was final. We lodged a Human Rights' complaint, and it didn't go anywhere before she allowed us in the next parade. We cancelled the complaint. That paved the way for other submissions in other parades. A testament to the power of education."

Carson clarified the timing, "Was this before Elaine Payne was mayor?"

"No, Barbara was elected mayor in 1995, two years after Elaine stepped down to run for federal politics. I'd say this took place around 1998 but I would have to look it up if you need it."

"OK, Andrew, what topic did you want to talk about?"

"Let's talk about taking our employer to task about equal rights benefits. After we came out to our friends and family, word spread quickly and verified what people at our place of work thought for years. No one ever asked us, they just spread rumours. I had been dealing with the federal Human Rights group about other issues and mentioned our company and equal rights. They told me that the telephone company was federally legislated and for that reason, had to have equal rights for LGBT employees. I checked with our health provider to see if we had health benefits and found out that we didn't. I asked how much it would cost to add them. They told me there was no additional cost, it just meant turning a switch on in the contract.

The company was a conservative place to work, but I needed to turn that switch on for all the LGBT people who didn't feel they could ask. I went to Human Resources, told them about what the federal Human Rights group had told me, gave them the name and phone number of the person I spoke with, and asked for the contract switch to be turned on. It took six months for them to get back to me with an emphatic 'no'. I heard that the company lawyer and the department head of Human Resources both said, 'yes' but the president said 'no'. I asked for the response to be put in writing and was told they wouldn't do that. I called Human Rights and explained the situation. They laughed and told me no company ever wants to put that in writing. They then asked if I wanted to lodge a complaint. I told her that the president had said 'no' so I needed to talk to him before I did that. I set up a meeting and asked the department head of Human Resources to attend.

The meeting was to last thirty minutes but ended up lasting two hours. It ended four times, each with the president reaffirming his no. Each time I told him we would have equal rights in the company, but I wanted him to say yes. I also told him that if he didn't put them in, I would. The meeting became quite tense at times,

Making A Difference

but I breezed through it because I was on the right side. He finally ended the meeting saying he wasn't saying *'no'* but he wasn't saying *'yes'*. He said he would leave it up to Ruth, the Human Resources Department Head. I reiterated that she and the company lawyer had both said, *'yes.'* but he was the one who said *'no'*. Throughout the interaction, Ruth hadn't said a word, so I turned to her and asked if she was comfortable with this situation. She was shaking when she said she was. Before leaving the office, the president said, *'Andrew, I don't agree with what you're doing but I admire the hell out of you for doing it.'*.

As we walked out, Ruth said she would like to meet with me so she would be educated on this request. We met weekly for a couple of months and during that time she asked me, *'Are you not concerned for your job?'* to which I responded, *'I have great performance reviews so if I get fired, I would be leaving here with the best retirement package anyone ever left with. Do you think I'd leave quietly?'* and she responded, *'No. I don't think you would.'* One day, I walked into her office for our meeting and, she told me the rights were in and added that I was to lay low.

I was happy I had achieved the equality I was looking for until a brochure about our benefits came out not mentioning same-gender couples. I went to Gregory and told him we needed to apply for couple benefits because I believed they hadn't done anything. I went to the manager who took my first request and delivered the company's *'no'* response. I told her I believed we were duped, and that Gregory and I were applying for couple benefits. I knew I was right when her response was, *'Andrew, please don't do this to me.'* It took them six more months before we were signed up for couple benefits. It was only then that I knew the switch hadn't been turned on."

They tackled one activity after the other over the rest of the day and into the evening. They called it quits near eight o'clock. They chatted into the evening about anything other than the book and all three were ready to get a good night's sleep by ten.

The three days were filled with great food and more stories and time whizzed by. When Carson left for home after supper on day three, he knew he would be working every day to get everything, they had talked about, written for the book."

Making A Difference

Chapter 23

Brock scanned the drawings, "These drawings are almost perfect!"

Matthew jumped on that statement, "Almost perfect? What doesn't work for you?"

Brock laughed, "It all works for me, but I just couldn't say it's perfect until I drill down on some of the details. Matthew, you have outdone yourself. I can't take my eyes off the entire rear wall being curved with large glass windows giving a panoramic view of the lake and gardens. I like that you have the kitchen area between the event pavilion and the art gallery for any catering that's needed, and the gallery has lots of hanging space for wall art and wide-open areas for sculpture. You seem to have thought of everything."

Matthew stood to the side so he could watch Brock's features as he commented on the drawings. He delighted in Brock's approval. After he explained the design nuances to Brock, he brought out a second set of drawings and rolled them out on a separate table. "This is the design of the whole property and details the gardens and how they fit in with the events pavilion, art gallery, and garden centre." He started pointing out different aspects of the design to Brock, "This pattern denotes the system of pathways throughout your park-like botanical gardens. There are benches on alternate sides depending on the view to be seen. I've planned five fountain areas, each with a specific theme. I have stone bridges over the four streams that feed the lake. We haven't talked about if the lake will be usable for paddle boats or whatever but that would be a simple design and if you want that, I suggest it will be at the end, away from the pavilion and off to the side. My first impulse is to keep it as a quiet and contemplative place."

Brock took it all in, "I like the arboretum at the back of the park area and that the gardens pathways lead to the garden centre. This is wonderful. Now I can say it's perfect, I wouldn't change a thing. When can the drawings for the pavilion and art gallery be ready for the developer?"

"There are just a few details I need to get approved by engineering, which shouldn't take very long. I expect you will have the finished drawings this time next week."

"So, I can take a set of these drawings so the developer can start planning the groundwork – right?"

Making A Difference

Matthew stood in a thoughtful pose, "Groundwork for positioning the parking lots, walkways and building placement would be fine. City Hall needs the drawings that detail the engineering when it's complete for the buildings."

"I promise I'll only be looking at placement of the design components. I'll see you next week." He turned to leave.

"Brock, can you stay a few minutes?" Matthew asked in a solemn voice.

Brock looked at Matthew with concern, "Is something wrong?"

"I wanted to let you know Dad has cancer and has started treatments. I'll be going with him for the first few to see how he'll handle them but mainly to support Mom. She's being brave for Dad's sake, but I know she isn't doing as well as she wants us to think. I wanted you to know."

"Thank you. If there is anything I can help with, let me know." He gave Matthew a tight hug.

Matthew let his guard down, "Thank you."

Brock felt the cold reserve had warmed, and he could now be a friend, "Are you seeing anyone?"

"Neal and I have hit it off since the dinner at the guys' cottage. He's really nice but so green. I've forgotten what it was like to be new to the gay scene. So many years have passed. How about you and Dirk, have you been a couple long?"

"Not long. I think we had been dating a week when you met him at dinner. His husband died a few years ago and I'm the first person he's dated since him. He still has periods of mourning and is processing through all that goes along with that."

Matthew swallowed hard, "I cannot even imagine what that must feel like. He's lucky to have you to help him through those tough times."

"Thank you. I know how hard it was when I lost Mammie and I go to that hurt when I try to understand his pain but mostly, I listen."

Matthew looked at the time, "This has been nice, I'm glad we can be friends. I have to run to another appointment now. I'll let you know when the drawings will be ready. I'll print off eight copies of each set." He walked him to the door and said goodbye. He watched as Brock walked to the car and drove off.

Sheila broke into his thoughts, "You have an appointment in fifteen minutes."

"Oh, God, I'm out of here. Thanks for the heads up."

*****

Making A Difference

When Matthew arrived, he was directed to go in Rich's office. When he heard someone approaching, Rich looked up, "Good morning, Matthew, how was your week?"

"It's been a different week. First thing, last session, I forgot to tell you that my dad has cancer. That makes me sad, but he's doing treatments and they say he has a good chance of beating it, but it's always at the back of my mind."

Rich jotted a note on his pad and addressed Matthew, "I'm sorry to hear that, and you're right, it will be part of everything you do. You seemed so happy with meeting Brock and expecting things to go back the way they were. How is the friendship going?"

Matthew paled and hesitated answering, "Brock is dating someone." He explained to Rich about being side swiped when Brock introduced Dirk as his boyfriend at the guys' dinner. He went on to tell him about Neal and how they have been dating.

Rich watched Matthew's reaction as he told his story, first sad that Brock had found someone new and happy when he talked about Neal. "How does Brock having a boyfriend make you feel?"

"It shocked me and deflated my expectation that we'd be together again."

"Would you say you were devastated?"

"I guess so. I really thought we were going to get back together. When he asked if we could be friends, I thought it was a done deal."

Rich thought for many long seconds before asking, "Is Neal a rebound boyfriend?"

"What do you mean?"

Rich leaned forward and spoke in calming tones, "You were so happy at the last session when you thought that you and Brock would get back together. When you told me about Brock's Dirk, your sadness was palpable. Is your Neal a distraction like all the guys you filled your life with after breaking up with Brock?"

Matthew paused as if he was formulating his answer, "Neal is a nice guy and I like being with him. Could it be a rebound relationship?"

"The way I see it, you're mourning that you and Brock will not be getting back together. The pain is evident to me. Rebound relationships often happen because the person is in denial and try to hide behind the new relationship, so they don't have to deal with the pain related to the breakup. I don't think you've dealt successfully with Brock's new relationship."

"Maybe. At the dinner party, I was hurt when I realized they were dating so instead of crying like I wanted to in that moment, I decided to focus my energy on possibilities and Neal was a definite possibility." Matthew's face reflected the realization that the words he spoke were more than he had entertained.

"You admit you were hurt. That is good."

Matthew lashed out, "What's so good about me being hurt?"

"I meant it's good you admitted the hurt. You have never said you hurt, you say you had regrets, you didn't feel fulfilled, you were resentful, you felt lost, and you said you were fucked up but at no time did you say you hurt. I'm glad you have finally admitted you hurt."

Matthew glared at Rich, "So, what does that revelation do for me?"

Rich took a moment, "OK, in our first session you said you felt lost. I sensed that feeling came from your quest for attention but finding the attention didn't ultimately fulfill you. At your core you want a relationship, but I want you to answer why you want one. Next session, I want us to dig down another layer and start to ask why you need a relationship. This isn't an easy question to answer so don't get frustrated; we'll get to the answer some day. In the meantime, I need you to ask yourself what all your one-night-stands really did for you."

"I'll give it a lot of thought, but I'm not sure I have the answers you're looking for."

Rich smiled, "I want you to be honest with yourself and the answers you find there will be the answers I want." He looked at the time, "OK Matthew, our time for today is up but I feel we're making progress. See you next week."

Making A Difference

Chapter 24

Brock walked through the front door of *'the manor'* and called out, "Honey, I'm home!" and went toward the kitchen.

Kaleisha was standing with her hands on her hips and a mischievous grin on her face, "You fool!" and walked toward Brock meeting him with a warm hug, "Fool or not, it's great to see you, I've so much to talk to you about for the wedding."

"Have you set a date and made your plans?"

"Roger and I have set Saturday, December 21st as the date. We'll have the place decorated for Christmas and I want you to do the garland with the lights that that couple had for their wedding on Valentines Day that you always talk about."

He grinned at her exuberance, "I've been working on it and you'll have the garland, I don't see any problems. The Christmas decorations go up just after the end of October so we can incorporate that design into this year's design. I'm assuming you have checked the date with the guys."

She smirked, "Of course I did, and they're fine. They really have so much free time on their hands now that they don't have to concern themselves with this place. They already have the food planned and are going to surprise me. They did ask if there was anything special that I wanted. I know whatever they plan will be wonderful, so I gave them free rein. I also told them Mom would be making a Jamaican dish which is a family favourite. She's arriving a week before the wedding, so she said she'd make it here."

"Is there anything I can do beyond the decorations. They'll be done early because of Christmas but there will also be some last-minute things that'll need to be done for the December 21st."

Kaleisha asked, "Brock, you're so organized. On the day of the wedding will you take over the logistics and manage the execution of the wedding, and the stand-up reception following the ceremony? If you will, I won't have anything to worry about."

Brock looked her in the eyes, "Definitely. I'll come early and leave late making sure everything goes according to plan. Over the next few months, we should sit and go step-by-step through everything that needs to be done. As for the actual ceremony, you have Andrew playing father of the bride and your son,

Making A Difference

Winston as Roger's best man so they'll be looking after that piece, but I'll manage who goes where and when. Who is standing up with you?"

"My daughter, Alvita. She's coming home for Christmas on Friday, the 20th. I hope she doesn't get delayed with a snowstorm."

"So much for not having anything to worry about." Brock laughed and gave her a hug.

They spent the next hour going over the plans Kaleisha made and talked about the plans that still needed to be made. They created a long list and when they hadn't come up with anything new, they called the list complete.

*****

Mackenzie was busy with some paperwork when Brock rapped on her door startling her into alertness, "Hey Bro, this is a surprise! What can I do for you?" She got up from her chair and hugged her brother.

"I was coming to see Dad about phase two of Pine Valley and thought I'd stop in and say hi."

"So, you must have gotten your drawings. That was fast."

Brock held up the two sets Matthew had given him, "There are a few things that need to be completed so Matthew thinks I should get the final ones next week. These will give Dad a really good idea of what we need to do. I'm hoping he agrees to take on the whole project. Do you have a room we could use for the next hour or so? I want to lay out the plans so Dad can see what the project entails."

Mackenzie got out a calendar and checked the date, "No one is using the board room today, you can use it as long as you like."

"Great, I'll go get Dad."

*****

Brock and Grant unrolled the plans for the event pavilion on one end of the table and the lake, gardens, and arboretum on the other end, "I call this the park area."

Grant spent several minutes digesting the designs, "This is a big job, when do you want to start?"

"I guess the real question is when do you think you could start."

"This shelter expansion should be close to completing within two months, but I could start on the permits and getting the crews lined up right away. You say we'll have final drawings next week?"

Making A Difference

"Yes, the engineering work will be done soon, and Matthew promised a final set next week. The ser for the park layout are complete so you may want to think of whatever permits you'll need to start that development. I'd like the buildings and the park area to be worked on in parallel if possible."

"Anything is possible, son, if we can find the work crews. The groundwork for the building should take priority and once the foundations are in place, then they can start creating the pathways for the park area."

"Are you saying you'll take this on?"

"Yes, Brock, I think this is an amazing project and I am honoured you asked me. I'm sure that within the next two weeks I'll have a better idea of what we need to do, get the trades on board, have the permits in place, and create a tentative schedule of what work will happen, and a timeline showing how the project will roll out. Let me know when you have the final drawings."

"Will do." He was about to roll the plans up when saw movement in his peripheral vision and looked to see what it was.

Mackenzie popped in, "I'm just too nosey to let you leave without knowing how the project will look. Take me through it."

Grant knew she would be into the details, so he excused himself, "I have to get back to work and get this expansion done. It looks like I just committed to, at least, a year's worth of additional work." He winked at both his children and left the room.

Mackenzie showed a keen interest in the design details and Brock loved showing her the drawings and explaining the nuances to her. She was amazed the pavilion was nestled in the park area facing the lake. She followed the pathways with her finger and commented on the stone bridges, gazebos, fountains, and the general layout of the park. This is beautiful, Brock. Saint John has nothing like this today. It's a good thing," she looked around to make sure no one was withing hearing distance, "you have lots of money."

"The gardens will have the trees and plants documented and people will be able to buy them at the garden centre. The arboretum will be planted with memorial trees. Families will pay for a tree and a plaque with the name of their loved one. I'm excited at the endless possibilities!"

Mackenzie faux punched his arm like they did when they were teenagers, "You, excited? No, that isn't possible!" She laughed, "All kidding aside, this is wonderful! I'm proud to be your sister. You're amazing!" She gave him a big hug. "Thanks for showing me this. I have a call I need to be on in five minutes. Gotta run!"

Making A Difference

Brock packed his drawings up and on his way to his car, he heard a horn. When he looked up, he spotted Dirk pulling over. "Hey hunk, what're you doing at the shelter?"

Brock hadn't said anything about his shelter involvement, so he responded, "My dad is doing the expansion and I needed to talk to him. Where are you headed?"

"I had to attend a business meeting, but I'm heading home right now. Why don't you come to my place for lunch?" Dirk said in a sultry voice and winked.

Brock caught the tone and excitement coursed through his veins, "You know, I'm ravenous. What are you serving?"

"Does it even matter? Let's say, I know you'll like it. Follow me!"

"I'll be right on your tail."

Dirk laughed, "You don't know how true those words will be. See you at home!"

Brock got in his car and followed thinking about the suggestiveness of their conversation. His mind flashed back to how Matthew was always horny, and the things he would say. He had to give his head a shake to clear Matthew out of his mind and focused on Dirk, his new, wonderful boyfriend.

When he arrived, Dirk greeted him at his car with a hug. "Come with me and see what I can come up with to deal with your ravenous nature." He took his hand and led an eager Brock inside.

Once the door was closed, Dirk and Brock locked their lips and kissed all the way to the bedroom shedding clothing in a haphazard array all along the hallway. They devoured each other's mouths while they dropped their pants and stood pressed together dressed only in silky boxer briefs which were straining to contain their lust. Brock freed himself from Dirk's talented tonguing and worked his way down Dirk's chest. He found the nipple and gently sucked it into his mouth all the while swirling his tongue around the hardened nib. Dirk allowed himself to relish the sensations and leaned his head into the wall behind to savour Brock's attention. They made their way to the bed, dropped the final garments, fell to the mattress, and gave each other the attention they desired. Hardness pressed against hardness and their readiness made their stomachs slick with their expectation. They undulated together in a dance of frenzied lust and exploded together as their moaning and exhalation reached the crescendo that culminated in their release. They lay together experiencing the resonance of their pounding hearts. They rolled together to their sides still facing each other, wrapped in each other's arms. Dirk looked into Brock's eyes and they both felt the special connection that only lovers do.

Making A Difference

Dirk spoke first, "I think I'm falling in love. I want to experience everything with you."

Brock felt the tenderness and tears ran down his face, "Dirk, you're so special to me and to say I love you seems to not do justice to this connection that we have. I cannot find words adequate enough."

"Maybe we'll discover our own words, words that have a special meaning only to the two of us. Brock, this scares me. I haven't opened myself up to anyone since Douglas. When he died, a piece of my heart died as well and only now do I feel fully alive again."

"I've tried with a couple of other guys, but no one measured up to Matthew. You have opened my heart again. I just have to learn to trust again. It hurt so much when he left me and that feeling colours everything. I like that you're open to discovering those words together."

Making A Difference

Chapter 25

Martha and Grant were in the final preparations for Sunday Family Supper. Today was special because both kids asked if their boyfriends could attend. They were looking forward to meeting Dirk and Tom, although Grant had a cursory meeting with Tom one day at the shelter.

As planned, Mackenzie and Tom picked up Brock and Dirk at Brock's place and arrived at their parent's home together. Introductions were made and Martha had laid out some appetizers for everyone to munch on while they became acquainted with each other. By the time supper rolled around, the air was filled with a level of familiar comfort. Awkward moments of silence were filled with camaraderie and soft laughter.

Dirk and Tom pitched in to take the numerous dishes to the dining table. On one trip, Tom commented, "I'm so going to enjoy this food. I know there is more coming, but I'm already impressed with the quantity and variety. I can hardly wait to dig in. Just in case anyone saw me sneak one of the pickled beets, I couldn't help myself. My grandmother used to make them, and my parents don't bother. Your beets taste just like hers. The smell made me take one."

One by one, they teased him about his confession and before long the table was laden with the meal. Martha, upon seeing the number of dishes said, "I think we went overboard. I kept thinking of the family favourites and I wanted" she looked first at Tom and then Dirk "you to experience them. Don't feel you have to eat everything. Enjoy!"

Grant said grace and they started passing dishes around and loading their plates. There were several minutes of quiet that normally follows people tasting their food, but conversation grew. They had learned how the shelter expansion was going and that Grant was going to start Brock's phase two of Pine Valley.

Upon hearing about Pine Valley, Tom perked up waiting to have his say, "That sounds like a wonderful project. Do you have the kind of trees the arboretum will have?"

Brock was pleased with Tom's question, "I'm looking at planting a large number of trees. I'll be working with the university to determine what kinds of trees I need and how many. There are several mature trees where I want the arboretum to be so maybe the university will tell me to keep some of those. It's a work in

Making A Difference

progress, and I expect I'll be working on it for years." He told Tom about working as the groundskeeper at *'the manor'* and that Andrew and Gregory had retired and now lived full-time in their cottage on the Kingston Peninsula. "Some day, we should take a drive so you could meet them and see their place."

Tom looked to Mackenzie, "Are these the same guys you worked for doing catering?"

Mackenzie responded, "Yes, Brock got me in for a New Year's Eve party when they needed people and I guess I proved myself because they hired me for many events after that. They're great guys, you'll love them. I haven't seen the cottage since they did the major renovation, so I'd like to stop in sometime. Maybe all four of us can go."

Dirk spoke up and explained he had been there for the dinner party for Neal but would like to go again."

"Who's Neal?", Mackenzie asked.

"A really nice gay man who installed the guys' internet and Gregory found he knew no one in the LGBT community but wanted to meet someone. The guys threw the party and invited eight people our age so Neal would be able to hang out and get to know the ropes, so to speak. He's now dating Matthew." Dirk explained.

"Those guys are so giving. If Neal never knew any LGBT people and he's now dating Matthew, that should really open his eyes. I understand through the grapevine, he's been quite the slut around town. Neal should be able to learn lots from him!" She paused and looked at her mom's horrified expression. "Don't get me wrong, I love Matthew. He's a wonderful guy, but I understand since he and Brock broke up, he wasted no time playing the field." All eyes went to Brock.

Brock blanched, it was easy to see he was hit hard by her words, "I didn't know. You'd think I'd have heard some hint from someone."

Mackenzie almost regretted what she said but she needed to say one more statement, "Bro, I didn't mean to offend you, but no one told you because you were carrying a big torch for Matthew for almost the whole four years. No one wanted to hurt you any further than you were hurting yourself."

The room went quiet as Brock digested what he had heard.

Grant broke the silence, "Brock, I see you copied all the documents. We'll need to get together and talk about where we go from here." He switched gears to avoid exposing too much, "Dirk, you say you grew up in the Fredericton area. Do your parents still live there?"

Making A Difference

"Yes, Dad is a police officer and Mom is an office manager. I have one brother, Jack, who is in Acadia University in Wolfville, Nova Scotia. Maybe some time when my parents come down this way, I could introduce you and Martha."

"We would like to meet them. How about you Tom, where did you grow up?"

"We moved a lot, but I see Truro as my hometown. That's where I graduated high school. My parents operate a corner store and I wanted to leave there before I got sucked into the business. My brother, Darren, will operate it when they retire in a few years. Now that Darren is well-versed in operating the business, Mom and Dad travel more so I'm expecting they'll be in Saint John soon to make sure I'm behaving myself. When they come, I'll have everyone over for supper."

Dirk acted as if Tom one-upped him, "Oh, thanks Tom, so I'm just introducing my parents, but you go and invite everyone to supper. That means I'll have a supper too." He went into a kids voice, "and mine will be better than yours! So there."

Everyone laughed and felt lightened by the humour.

They moved into the living room and the Mathesons regaled Tom and Dirk with enough family stories to bore most people but both guys put on a good front until Mackenzie turned the tables and had them tell more of their stories. All in all, it made for an informative night.

*****

Mackenzie and Tom left with Brock and Dirk and all four talked outside Brock's place making tentative plans for the visit with Andrew and Gregory. Brock agreed to set the date and get back to everyone.

As Tom walked Mackenzie home he asked, "Does this count as our second date?"

She was confused with the question and remembered his words about not going too far on the first date. "I could be persuaded to make this the second date, but it doesn't seem romantic to count a family dinner as a date."

Her words didn't deter Tom, "When we get to your place, I'll persuade you like no one ever persuaded anyone before. You want romantic, I'm your guy!"

Mackenzie did her famous faux punch and teased him, "I can hardly wait to see how you make tonight romantic. That's your challenge should you choose to accept it."

"You're on!"

Making A Difference

As Mackenzie was unlocking her door, Tom went to his car saying, "I'll be back in a minute. You had better slip into something more comfortable and ready for romance."

Mackenzie giggled to herself. She loved Tom's playful side and she was looking forward to whatever was going to happen next. She heard music but couldn't make out what song it was. It was getting louder and louder and soon Tom was standing in her living room with his phone playing her favourite love song, holding a bouquet of red roses, and a bottle of her favourite wine. The music played while Tom went around the room turning lights down or off and lighting candles. He presented her with the roses and followed her to the kitchen. She tried to arrange the roses, but Tom was busying himself with gently kissing the nape of her neck. She squirmed and giggled but loved it. She gave into his ministrations, and he took her hand and led her to the sofa while he carried two wine glasses in the other hand. She sat on the couch, and he opened the wine and filled a glass which he passed her. He sat and they intertwined their arms and took a sip.

"You were up for this challenge, and you have succeeded. I'm loving you and your spontaneous ideas and if you play your cards right...."

Tom stopped her saying anything more by kissing her and she gave in. They tempted and tasted each other and began to undo buttons. He plied her neck with soft kisses and nibbled at her ear and tongued behind them. He opened her blouse and kissed her breasts unhooking her bra so he could let both of her breasts rest in his hands. He continued kissing and played with both nipples with his thumbs while she moaned. When he bent to suck one nipple into his mouth, she squealed in pleasure and when he tongued it, she let her inhibitions go. She could feel his excitement with the side of her leg and reached to undo his belt and zipper. His lust filled her hand, and she knew she wanted more. Raising up from the couch, Tom looked at her with puzzlement until she rid herself of her jeans and panties. She then lowered herself onto his rigidness and, facing him, kissed his mouth. Using her well-exercised thighs, she raised and lowered herself and Tom began sucking her nipple. He licked a finger and found her clitoris.

Mackenzie came alive, "Oh God, Oh God, Oh God!" She screamed louder and louder and she exploded. He lifted her off just in time to explode. They lay in each other's arms and brought their breathing under control.

Tom looked at her, "We never talked about condoms. I had one in my pocket but you took me by surprise. I had a hard time holding my orgasm off, but I got out in time."

Making A Difference

"I'm on the pill and from what you've told me, neither of us have been sexually active for a while so we're practically virgins. I assumed we were safe."

Tom looked her in the eyes, "Was it romantic enough?"

"Oh Tom, that was very romantic. You are a special man!"

Making A Difference

Chapter 26

Grant, Brock, Martha, and Mackenzie met in the lobby of the office tower. Brock explained, "Axel Godrey has a law firm, on the fourteenth floor, which specializes in lawsuits against large organizations. He comes highly recommended and when I spoke with him, he seemed enthusiastic about Father Mike's documentation but wants to have a look at it before committing. I sent the material over and it's waiting with the receptionist."

Martha commented, "Wouldn't any lawyer be enthusiastic if they saw money in the lawsuit?"

Grant looked at her, "Honey, no need to be cynical. Brock has done his research and I feel we need to give this lawyer a look. We do know he won't be cheap."

"Usually, these lawyers will take a case on when they feel they have a good chance to win, and they get their costs paid as part of the settlement."

The elevator stopped on the fourteenth floor, and they made their way to the lawyer's firm. The nameplate on the receptionist's desk informed them his name was Liam. When Brock gave his name, Liam pointed to two boxes next to his desk. "These arrived for you, I'll make sure they'll be taken into the conference room where you'll be meeting with Mr. Godfrey. Please take a seat and he will be out for you shortly."

They took seats and chatted amongst themselves when a well-dressed man came out, introduced himself as Axel Godfrey, and asked them to call him Axel. He led them to a conference room and as they took their seats, Liam brought the two boxes in on a rolling cart leaving them and the cart together off to the side. Brock introduced his family to the lawyer and explained what the contents were.

"I'll have a look at the documents in a few minutes but first, I want you to elaborate on what you're hoping to achieve by going ahead with this lawsuit?"

Grant spoke up, "Father Mike was a local priest here in Saint John who abused me when I was a kid. He was caught by the bishop while abusing another boy and was sent away. As part of my healing I went to St. John's, Newfoundland and Labrador several years ago to confront him about the abuse. When we met, he gave me a letter he wrote me which he intended to be delivered to me after his death. At that time, he showed me a shoebox full of letters to other children he had

Making A Difference

abused. We had a frank conversation and I left feeling I succeeded in confronting him. I thought it was done and over but during the pandemic, he succumbed to Covid19, and the boxes of documents were delivered to me as part of his estate. You'll see he documented abuse in the Catholic church over the years. My desire is to help make a difference in the lives of the victims by taking the Church to task. They knew it was happening and didn't do enough to protect the kids who came into contact with those abuser priests. I want them to pay."

Axel took notes as he listened to Grant's story, "And when you say pay, what kind of payment are you looking for?"

Grant had thought about that many times and answered, "I know what it's like to live with being taken advantage of sexually and be afraid to tell anyone. It ruined my life and almost my family until I dealt with it. I want the Church to compensate the adults who were the priests' victims and help them heal, whatever those costs are. It isn't OK by any standard for the Church to get away with hiding behaviours which hurt people."

"There is a history of abuse in the Catholic Church that has been dealt with in court and many suits have been successful. I'll compare the type of evidence you have with the evidence which helped win those other cases." He looked at the others, "How about the rest of you, do you agree with Grant's answer?"

All heads nodded and Brock added, "Dad is the main player and if that's what he wants, we agree with his assessment."

Axel smiled, "So let's see what you have here." He placed one box on the table and started to remove packets documents, "Can someone explain what guidelines you used to organize the evidence the way you did?"

Mackenzie took the lead and explained her methodology and used one of the groups to help illustrate what they had done.

Axel showed his surprise, "Your work will make our job easier. I'll take some time and study what you have done and determine our course of action. Are there any questions?"

"How soon do you think we can meet again with that determination?" Grant asked.

"I think I'll put my team on this work, and we should be able to come up with a tentative plan within three weeks. Can we book a meeting three weeks out at one o'clock?"

Everyone reached for their phones and within minutes they had it in their calendars.

Making A Difference

*****

Matthew and his mother sat in the waiting room of the oncology department waiting for his father to finish his chemotherapy. Today will be his last session and then they'll wait for him to be tested to see how it worked. His mother didn't look well, and she was nodding off on his shoulder, "Mom, how are you really doing? You always answer that everything is going well but you look exhausted."

Bonny forced a weak half-smile, "I'm tired, but I don't want your dad to worry about me. He has enough to deal with taking these cancer treatments. I can't seem to stay asleep. When I hit the pillow and I'm out like a light, but I wake a couple of hours later usually to go pee and when I get back to bed, I think all night long. Then I start watching the clock and trying to will myself back to sleep but it seldom works. I'm hoping that when the treatments are done, he gets an *'all clear'* and we don't have to worry about it."

"Mom, you need to take care of yourself."

"I will, don't you worry about me." Bonny looked past Matthew and starred out the window into the garden deep in thought. "How's your new boyfriend?"

"Neal is so new to being gay that I think I scare him. He's a really sweet guy, and we're continuing to get to know each other. One thing I do know is it isn't right for me to compare him to Brock. It just isn't fair to him, but it's an automatic reaction. I've done it to my other boyfriends, and we can see how those relationships turned out."

"You still love him, don't you?" Bonny looked at him with eyes that spoke of the sadness she felt in his story.

"Mom, I do. I try to not love him, but I can't stop. We've not been together for four years now and I hadn't talked much to him, I avoided him because I screwed up and have regrets. Last month, I went to the garden centre pretending to need a plant, but I really wanted to see if we could get back together. He was friendly and I got my hopes up but then I went to dinner at Andrew and Gregory's cottage, and he was there with his new boyfriend, Dirk. Talk about a slap in the face. I tried not to show my hurt and I directed my attention to the others. I ended up talking to Neal and that's how we got together."

"I can hear it in your voice, Neal doesn't measure up to Brock. Maybe you need to let go of the hope of getting back together with him and find out how wonderful Neal is when you don't compare him to anyone else. You need to bring him by someday so your dad and I can meet him." She didn't say another word until Doug's nurse informed them he was ready to go.

Making A Difference

They took Doug home and got him comfortable. They chatted a little, but Doug drifted off to sleep.

Matthew and his mom prepared lunch and they sat at the table. As they ate, she tried another tactic, "Matthew, how about you bring Neal over some night for supper?" She didn't see any excitement, so she finished with, "At least think about it. Don't give up so fast."

Matthew acknowledged her comment, "OK Mom, I'll consider it and let you know." He finished his meal and announced, "I'm going to get back to work now." He hugged her and spoke gently into her ear, "I love you, Mom."

"I love you too, Honey."

*****

Matthew was working on a new design when Neal texted, *'Hey Matthew, what are U up 2 tonight?'*

'I was just about to text U. Anson just invited us for supper for 6 tonight. R U up for that?'

'Sure, can we bring anything?'

'Anson says they have everything planned. Charles has even made a surprise dessert! I think we can take some wine.'

'I'll pick it up on the way over. Do U want me to go to your home or meet U at Anson and Charles' place?'

Matthew hesitated, thinking about his mom's conversation, *'Why don't U come to my home, and we can go over together.'*

'K, C U at 5:30.'

*****

Matthew thought about his mother's conversation all afternoon. When he got home, his dad was in a good mood and he told his mom that Neal was picking him up, "Is tonight a good time to meet him?"

Bonny was thrilled, "Yes! Will he stay for supper?"

Matthew smiled, "Not tonight, Mom, we're invited out tonight, but I think it's a great idea. When would be good?"

She offered some suggestions, "Maybe you could invite him when you meet him."

The doorbell announced Neal's arrival. Matthew opened the door and asked, "I'd like you to come in so you could meet Mom and Dad, are you good with that?"

Making A Difference

Neal's face lit up, "I've been waiting for you to suggest this for weeks now. I want to meet them."

Matthew took Neal into the living room where his parents were sitting, and he made the introductions. Bonny engaged Neal in conversation and Doug asked about his parents and what he did for a living. Neal was comfortable with the questioning and when they left to go over to Anson & Charles' place for supper, he commented, "When you didn't introduce me, I thought there must be something you were afraid for me to see, but they seem very normal. I'm glad I met them."

Matthew opened up as they walked, "It wasn't them; it was me."

"What do you mean?"

"I haven't had much luck in the relationship arena since Brock so I hesitated showing my parents one more boyfriend who would eventually leave me. I sometimes feel like a failure"

Neal stopped and turned toward Matthew, "Matthew, I like who you are and, although I have no experience, I want us to work toward a relationship if you're willing."

"I didn't know I was until today." He explained the conversation he had with his mother and the advice she gave him, "Would you like to be my boyfriend?"

"Matthew, I thought you would never ask! Yes, I'd love to be your boyfriend. I've been hesitating to ask you to do things because I sensed you weren't into me. I'm new to the gay world, and I don't think I'm ready for my first failed relationship."

"That's my fault and I apologize. I've had such a defeatist attitude lately and I didn't think you would want me. Let's leave that all behind and put our energies into becoming a couple."

"I'll do this as long as you open up to me, so I know what you're thinking. Deal?"

"Deal!"

Making A Difference

Chapter 27

Gregory and Andrew left the cottage dressed in warm clothing for the breezy late September weather. When they moved in, they started a daily routine that included a five-kilometre walk. The sun created vibrant displays when it backed the vibrant reds, oranges, and yellows of the fall colours. The traffic was light, and they waved to the people they knew who drove by and even people they didn't know. The Kingston Peninsula was just that sort of place. Gregory let the sun warm his face and offered, "I'm glad we started these walks; I feel they boost my energy for the rest of the day."

Andrew was relishing the leaf colours and pointed to the things he noticed, "Look at how that cluster glows. Nature is really amazing." He went to add something else when he saw Gregory's body rolling by on the hood of a red car as the side mirror brushed his elbow. His first instinct to go after the car but it hit a tree and threw Gregory deeper into the trees. He stumbled down the ditch, pushed his way through the bushes, and followed screams of pain where he found Gregory trying to get up. "My leg is hurting like hell. I think it's broken."

Andrew found his phone, but he was shaking so hard he could barely dial 911. He connected with the dispatcher and explained Gregory's injuries. He answered questions with Gregory's help about his condition, and they said they would send an ambulance. The dispatcher then asked about the driver of the car. A stunned Andrew replied, "I was so concerned about Gregory, I haven't left his side. I'll go to the car now."

He climbed out of the bushes up a steep incline to get to the car. The driver, a huge man, took up most of the driver's side and was slumped over the wheel. He got the door open and checked to see if the man was alive. The dispatcher asked Andrew several questions and determined they needed two ambulances. Andrew went in through the passenger's door and turned the engine off. He noticed a couple of blankets in the back seat so he wrapped one around the driver as best as he could and took one to Gregory to keep him warm. He stayed on the line and answered questions as the call progressed. The RCMP arrived first followed shortly by the firefighters, and then the first ambulance. The paramedics did an assessment of both the driver and Gregory and deemed the driver may have had a heart attack, so they decided to take him first. The second ambulance arrived

Making A Difference

as they were loading him onto a stretcher. They gave the second paramedics a brief assessment of Gregory's condition before leaving. They took their equipment into the bushes, strapped Gregory onto a body board as he sucked air through his teeth with the pain. They carried him up the slope and got him into the ambulance.

Andrew told Gregory he would get their car and meet him at the *'Outdoor'*. He stood watching as the ambulance drove off and disappeared around a corner just as a tow truck arrived. While the driver was getting the car ready for transport, the RCMP offered him a lift back to the cottage. On the way the Mountie told him it looked like the driver had a heart attack and his foot must have fallen off the accelerator. That probably saved Gregory's life because the car was rolling off the road slower than it could have been. At the cottage, his mind went into overdrive, and he gathered things he thought they would need at the hospital.

As he drove in, he replayed talking to Gregory one second and his body flying past him. He was concerned for Gregory and was thankful the car wasn't a little farther over or they could both have broken bones or worse. He then thought about the driver and wondered if he had passed out at the wheel causing him to drive off the road.

He found Gregory in a room with Dr. Bennett, according to his name tag, going over his chart. Andrew patted Gregory's arm and introduced himself to the doctor and asked about Gregory's pain. "Do we know what has happened yet?"

Dr. Bennett shook his head, "We don't know for sure, but Gregory thinks the leg is broken so I'm sending him for x-rays. They are coming to get him now and he should be back here in half an hour." He finished that sentence and a PSW arrived to take him.

Andrew played games on his iPad while he waited and before long, they were rolling Gregory back into the room. The attendant said, "The doctor is looking at the x-rays now and should be in soon."

Andrew went to the bedside and rubbed his arm, "How are you feeling? Is the pain bearable?"

"The leg is the worst, but my arm is really sore too. They gave me some drugs, so I still feel pain, but it isn't as intense." Gregory winced as he spoke.

Dr. Bennet entered, "Well Gregory, you diagnosed it correctly. Your leg is broken mid calf, but your arm is only severely bruised. We need to get a cast on the leg, and you'll need to stay off it for six to eight weeks. Your arm will be black and purple for a while, it will just need time. I'll go make arrangements for your cast."

"I called the kids while you were getting your cast put on. They were ready to come up but I told them you would be released soon. I invited them to come for

Making A Difference

supper, but they called back and suggested they bring the food. We're having Chinese!"

By late afternoon, Gregory was discharged. While he was getting his cast, Andrew went out and bought crutches. A physio therapist popped in to see Gregory's leg and set up an appointment. He encouraged Gregory to get out of bed, made sure they were adjusted, and showed him how to use them to keep his weight off his leg. With that, and a prescription for pain killers, they were ready go home.

Gregory stayed in the car while Andrew filled the prescription at the Costco pharmacy. While waiting for the drugs, he picked up food items he knew they needed, a selection of treats Gregory would like, a urinal for convenience, and several magazines.

At home, Andrew held doors and, once Gregory was settled, he created a convalescent oasis of items he could use as he healed.

Gregory looked around, "You've thought of everything. I'm going to be laying low for a while. Did you find out what happened?"

Andrew hesitated, "The Mountie told me the driver did have a heart attack and he doesn't remember anything but driving and then waking in the hospital. You were hit by a car with no active driver but if the car had been over a little, we could have both been killed."

"I've been thinking about today and how fast things can make a difference to our lives. I count myself lucky."

"That's one way to look at it."

Gregory heard something and cocked an ear, "I hear a car, are the kids here?"

Andrew went to the window and saw all three of their kids, their spouses, and their children, "The whole gang is here."

The cottage filled with worried voices until Gregory helped them understand he wasn't dying. The concern was replaced with lively chatter interspersed with giggles and laughter. Gregory was wearing a T-shirt and the grandchildren took an interest in the colourful bruising and the smallest wanted to have his arm painted as well.

The food was soon laid out on the island, and everyone loaded their plates and found a place to eat. Andrew got a plateful for Gregory and took it to him in the living area. Some of the kids, seeing this, took their food and ate with him so he wouldn't be left out.

*****

Making A Difference

Brock walked in followed by Dirk carrying a beautiful flower arrangement. They called out in unison, "We brought these to cheer up the invalid!" Dirk set the arrangement on the table next to Gregory. They each hugged him, and Brock asked, "Where's Andrew?"

Gregory told them he had gone in town to get some supplies, "I've been craving mint chocolate ice cream, and I planted the seed. I'm hoping he took the hint, and my craving will be satisfied when he gets here."

Brock wanted to know, "He had let me in on what happened, but I'd like to hear your account."

"Well, Andrew was eyewitness, so I expect he has the better story. All I know is we were walking and talking, and I was hit from behind and sailed with the car until it hit a tree sending me flying into the bushes. Andrew called 911 and I ended up in the '*Outdoor*' where I got x-rayed and casted."

"That's pretty well what he told me. How are you feeling?"

"The pain is dulled by the medication, but it's still there, though not debilitating."

Dirk broke in, "So how long will you be laid up?"

Gregory smirked, "Well, they say six to eight weeks as long as I stay off my feet. They said rest heals best and I want to get this over with, so I'll not be putting any weight on that foot. Kaleisha's wedding is in December, and I need to be walking around by then."

Brock did some mental calculation, "That's twelve weeks away so you should be fine. She has most of the plans set and her kids and mom are coming. It should be a great evening."

They heard a car and Gregory's eyes lit up, "That's Andrew. Any bets on me getting ice cream?"

Dirk answered, "Knowing how you two have impressed me with your relationship, my money is on him having it!"

Andrew walked in with three bags and announced, "Guess what I bought?" He held up the chocolate mint ice cream and all three laughed. "Alright, you guys, something just happened, and I need to know."

Brock filled him in, "All bets were on you buying the ice cream and you came through."

Gregory, asked, "Would anyone like a dish?"

Hands went up all round and, while Andrew put the groceries away, Brock dished out the four bowls and passed them around. They sat, ate and chatted through the afternoon.

Making A Difference

Andrew noted the time, "Will you stay for supper?"

Dirk responded, "We don't want to be a bother."

"Bother, I know you're both great cooks, so I was going to let you cook."

Everyone laughed, and Andrew took them through the ingredients he had available, and they went to work while Andrew sat with Gregory, and he filled him in on the things he saw in town.

At supper, Brock brought up the shelter's expansion, "The work is almost done for the expansion, and Dad is working between there and my Pine Valley development. How are you guys feeling about the shelter?"

Andrew perked up, "This was an easy project to do. It's almost like we picked up where we left off seven years ago, so we didn't mind it at all. Having your dad on board made our job super easy."

One afternoon about twenty good friends and family members showed up for an impromptu party to celebrate Andrew and Gregory's fortieth anniversary of being together. They brought gifts and food and created a party atmosphere that both guys enjoyed.

Having regular visits made the time go faster than Gregory had expected the first month would go. It seemed to fly by and there were milestones. He became skilled at manoeuvring with the crutches, and he reclaimed his independence by doing chores and making meals. He even tried shopping but found he tired too easily so he let Andrew do the bulk of it. Gregory was determined to be healed as fast as he possibly could, so he followed the doctor's orders to the letter.

Making A Difference

Chapter 28

Bonny took the afternoon off from work and planned to have everything ready when Neal came for supper. She hummed an upbeat tune as she worked around the kitchen and set the table. She was the happiest Matthew had seen her since his dad was diagnosed with cancer. "You seem to be cheery today, are you so thrilled that Neal is coming for supper or is there something special I need to know about?"

"Your dad got his test results today and there is no evidence of any cancer. He will be tested again in three months and if that's still good, he goes into six-month appointments with his oncologist." As she explained, he noticed his mom couldn't keep still.

Matthew was surprised, "I didn't think we would get the results so soon. Dad has to be pleased."

"He is more than pleased. It's like he had been given a whole new lease on life."

"In a way, that's what he's been given." He looked over at the pots on the stove, "What's for supper?"

"I have a roast in the oven, and we're having garden vegetables. I even made rolls!"

"If that's the kind of food he's getting, I should have invited Neal over long before this!" Matthew winked at his mother.

"You're bad. I wanted to celebrate Dad's great news and Neal just happened to be coming for supper. It just worked out! What's new in your world, Son?"

"Not a whole lot. Did you hear about Gregory getting hit by a car while they were out for their morning walk?"

"No, I hadn't heard. Is he OK?"

Matthew explained how the accident happened and how Gregory was doing, "Neal and I went out to visit and he's doing very well. He's fiercely independent, and he wants to make sure he heals so he can be ready for catering Kaleisha's wedding. It's their gift to Kaleisha and Roger. I don't have any doubts he'll be there."

"That's a wonderful gift! Every married couple should be so lucky."

"Work is really busy. One of Anson's clients needs a subdivision designed and he isn't interested in a cookie-cutter approach. It's a great challenge and we've put ten designs with multiple layouts for each design in our proposal. The client loved the flexibility and hired us, so we have to deliver the subdivision plan by the end of the year."

Bonny looked concerned, "Will it keep you busy?"

Matthew nodded, "The project is huge, but we also have several others on the go so we have more work than we really need but with some extra hours, we'll deliver on all of them. I think I'll be able to move into my own apartment."

"How are you doing with Brock? You haven't mentioned him much since we talked."

"We're good. When we talked, I realized I was holding out for Brock and not investing in my relationship with Neal. I wasn't being fair to either of us, and you were the one who opened my eyes." Just then the doorbell rang, "There is Neal now." As he went to the door, he left the room with, "So, you were what I needed to finally let go of Brock and commit to Neal."

As Neal entered, he kissed Matthew and hugged him saying, "I've missed you so much today and I looked forward to seeing you tonight."

Matthew was surprised but pleased. He did not have any hesitation with Neal as his boyfriend, "You'll have to tell me about your day and what caused you to miss me sometime when we're alone."

Matthew and Neal went into the living room, had a small chat with Doug, and ended up in the kitchen talking with Bonny. She asked Neal how his day had gone, and he kept his answer light although he did explain at length a piece of technology he was now installing until he saw her eyes glaze over, "I'm sorry, this is way too technical. I love learning new things, but I sometimes don't realize everyone isn't on the same wavelength."

Bonny tried to downplay his concern, "I think I was getting it. That thingy you were talking about had something to do with the internet running better, right?"

"I think you got the gist of what I was saying but I could have stayed away from all the technical jargon to make it simpler to understand. I'm giving you points for being able to weed through everything and still get the basic meaning of it. Bravo Mrs. Erb."

"Well, supper is almost ready. I just have to make the gravy and we'll be able to eat."

Neal jumped in, "How can we help?"

"Well, you both could drain the vegetables and get them in serving dishes while I do the gravy. Matthew, would you make your special whipped potatoes? Dad really likes them the way you do them?"

Making A Difference

Everyone worked together, and the food was ready to go to the table when Doug joined them, "It looks like I came at the right time." He took the platter of roast beef and the rolls with him. "Let's go!"

As everyone took their seats, they joined hands in an unbroken circle and Doug said grace. Amid the clanging of serving spoons as the food was passed around, they enjoyed mindless chatter. Soon everyone's plate was full and a quiet enveloped the room. As they got their first forkfuls swallowed, the chatter ensued.

Matthew looked across the table to Neal's smiling face and watched as he conversed back and forth between his parents. He took his foot and stretched across under the table to rub Neal's leg. He was in love.

*****

As conversation moved into the kitchen, everyone helped with the cleanup and moved into the living room. As the night wore on, Doug began to appear tired, so Matthew suggested, "Mom and Dad, the meal was so tasty. You're both tired so Neal and I will leave so you can go to bed."

Neal hugged both of Matthew's parents, "Thank you so much for the wonderful supper and nice evening of conversation. I wish I had a place so I could have you over to repay your kindness."

Bonny looked at Matthew and winked but hid it from Neal, "In time you will, and I look forward to that day."

*****

When they drove off in Neal's car, Matthew suggested, "Let's drive out to Mispec Park and walk along the beach in the moonlight."

"I would love that."

They chatted about their day and got to the park sooner than expected. They took the stairs and walked down to the water's edge with the tide coming in. Matthew wanted to know, "When you kissed me you mentioned you missed me all day, I'd love to hear this story. Are you ready to share?"

"Yes, I'm very ready. I know we've only known each other for a few months, and I don't have the experience you have but the feelings I have for you are strong and they invade my mind all the time. Today, when I was thinking about you, I'd lose my concentration. I must have looked like an idiot because I'm sure I had a dumb smile on my face. I guess what I'm trying to say is I love you."

"Neal, I love you too. It took me a while to clear my head to open myself up to you, but I have no doubts. I really love you."

Making A Difference

They embraced and kissed. Neal suggested, "There's a private rock ledge surrounded by trees over around that outcropping, would you like to come with me?" He winked.

Matthew smiled as he heard the message, "I'd love to come with you."

They walked along the water and found Neal's secret ledge. It radiated warmth from the afternoon sun which took away the night's chill. They used their jackets for padding against the rock surface and lay down facing each other chatting and kissing. They embraced. The combined warmth from the heat of the ledge and their bodies allowed more clothing to be removed in the moonlight with their slow sensual exploration. Matthew didn't feel rushed and took Neal on a journey of pleasure. As they neared their climaxes, they allowed themselves to free their voices with no fear of anyone hearing. They lay in each other's arms relishing in their chests and stomachs being pressed together and allowing their breathing to return to normal.

Matthew broke the silence, "Neal, I feel we need more times like this, would you agree?"

Neal looked into his shadowed face, "I agree, we do need private time. Having no place to go has been a challenge from the start."

"If we moved in together and shared the costs, we could afford a place of our own. Would you like that?"

"Oh Matthew, I'd like that a lot. We'd need a two bedroom so my parents would think we were roommates until I get up the nerve to tell them. I don't see that happening any time soon though."

"As long as we're together, everything else will happen when it needs to. Do you want to start looking tomorrow?"

"Hell, I'm going to be looking tonight."

They each agreed to compile a list of prospects and together decide which ones they would want to see and then make appointments for the coming evenings. They decided to look in the uptown area so Matthew could walk to work. By the next evening, they had six prospects and appointments for the next day. They developed a list of the must haves like off-street parking for Neal's car, and two bedrooms and the nice to haves like street-level entrance, and a back yard. They decided to use a grid to assess each of the apartments.

*****

After a full night of viewing apartments, they easily narrowed it down to two and sat discussing the pros and cons of each one. They had taken pictures and

Making A Difference

used those shots to compare aspects of both in their deliberations. They chose a spacious, sunny, ground-floor, two-bedroom, two-bathroom apartment in a well-maintained 135-year-old building on Queen Square South. It had ten-foot ceilings, hardwood floors, original mouldings, a working fireplace, and great architectural details. It even had a storage shed they could put their bicycles in. They met with the landlord, signed the lease, and paid the first month's rent. Their move-in date was the end of October. The current tenants were moving on the twenty-eighth into their new home so the landlord said she would allow Matthew and Neal to start moving in then.

Chapter 29

Brock watched with his father as the cement trucks were pouring the footings for the pavilion and art gallery. "It always amazes me how small new builds look at this stage."

Grant agreed, "Yes, it fools many people, but I can assure you this is the size of the building in your blueprints."

"I would like this to be completed for the end of June next year, is that possible?"

"If that's what you want, I can put extra crews on to make sure we're done. What's going on the end of June?"

"I nominated Andrew and Gregory for a Governor General's Order of Canada for all of the work they did for LGBT rights and same-gender marriage. Next year is the twentieth anniversary of the court case where they and three other couples took the province of New Brunswick to court to make same-gender marriage legal. I'd like to hold a celebration right here for the anniversary and, hopefully, them receiving their award." Brock looked at the cement and tried to picture the finished building. "I wish I had a better sense of how long things should take."

Grant wanted Brock to know how he was playing out the design., "The grounds crew have walked the property with the blueprints and are focusing on the botanical gardens that butt up against the garden centre and the arboretum and extending the gardens up and around the lake. You should be able to plant some of it soon for next year's growth while the rest will be done in the spring. We do have the lake area plantings in front of the pavilion and the surrounding planters bordering the parking lots as a priority so it should look good when you open for business."

"That sounds great. I'm ordering all the plants for those areas, so they'll be delivered on time to plant in the spring. Do you have any free time that we could go over to the shelter and see how things are finishing up there?"

"Sure, I'll meet you there after I talk to the foreman." Grant walked onto the site and up to one of the workers.

*****

Making A Difference

Brock was talking to Mackenzie and Tom when Grant arrived. Brock summarized, "As I understand the work being done to minimize disruption, the rooms in the addition will be completed before you cut the hole for the staircase. How far off before that's done?"

Grant went into his calculation mode, "I think we'll be cutting the staircase this Friday and it's already sitting up there waiting. It will be manoeuvred into place on Monday of next week and supported so it can be welded. We'll need another week to put the final touches on everything and then Mackenzie will let us know if there are any glitches, but we should be able to increase capacity in three weeks at the latest."

"So then, everyone will be working at Pine Valley pavilion." Brock was smiling.

"We can use some of them for the general construction, but the finish crews won't be needed for months yet. Why don't you three put on hard hats and have a look around?"

They got the hats and used the elevator to go to the expansion area. The rooms were painted but missing trim. Mackenzie checked out each one and marveled at how similar they were to the first residential floor. "This looks like it'll be done before three weeks."

Grant nodded, "I'd say you're right; they seem to be ahead of schedule. I'll speak with the foreman and see where we stand" He left the three looking over the area and was back in minutes, "The stairs will be installed tomorrow, so we'll easily be done in two weeks. The outside was completed today and there is just the inside to finish off. I have to get back at the pavilion, so I'll see you and Brock tomorrow for our meeting and Tom, I'll see you on Sunday for our family supper."

As Grant walked away, Brock hit his forehead with the palm of his hand, "I almost forgot, I contacted Andrew and Gregory and we're invited out for supper next Tuesday."

Mackenzie nodded, "I'm glad you remembered. We still have it open. Do we want to travel together?"

Tom spoke up, "Might as well all go in my car. I'm looking forward to meeting them."

*****

Making A Difference

The four Mathesons had just arrived and were seated in the lawyer's waiting room, when Axel Godfrey came out from the conference room, greeted them and asked them to follow him.

In the conference room, Axel reviewed the work they had done and explained, "Father O'Hara was very thorough in collecting the evidence. I think we have enough here to make the case, but I'd recommend we have testimony from the victims. Can you contact any of the victims mentioned in the documents?"

Brock looked to his father, "I thought we weren't going to go this route." He looked to his mother, "Mom, you were adamant we wouldn't cause anyone any more pain."

Axel saw where the mood was going and stepped in, "If they chose to participate, isn't that up to the individual? The case will have more power if we put the human element in it. Grant, you said that Father O'Hara abused you so if you're willing, you can start the case and we could do a news story about the case and ask people to come forward. How does this feel?"

Martha leaned on the table and looked directly at Axel, "As long as they volunteer and are not forced, I'd be OK with having the victims participate. Grant, how do you feel about leading the charge?"

"I'm OK with me being in the forefront. I've read a lot when I was doing my research and people can get stuck because of the abuse and feeling powerless to do anything about it. Think about all the people this will help."

Mackenzie spoke up, "We need to find someone who will write the story and get it out there. Brock, didn't you say there's a reporter writing about Andrew and Gregory?"

Brock nodded, "His name is Carson Drummond, and I could approach him about this."

Axel listened, "We can make this a class action suit against the Catholic Church and as more people come forward, we add them to the list. How soon do you think we could talk to the reporter?"

"I'll call later today and see what he says."

*****

Carson was interviewing Andrew and Gregory when Brock called Andrew so he asked if Carson would speak with Brock.

Brock told Carson the story of Father Mike and his abuse of Grant. He took him through receiving the two boxes of documentation and what the lawyer said about it. He kept him on the line for half an hour when Carson broke in,

Making A Difference

"Brock, I'm very interested. I need to pass it by my editor, and I'll get back to you. Can I reach you at this number?"

Brock assured him he would always have his phone with him. He was sitting in Mackenzie's office, and she waited for him to finish the call. He shared what Carson said and summed it up. "Now we wait."

Mackenzie opened up about her relationship with Tom and how happy she was. Brock shared his relationship with Dirk. They were generally talking about how lucky they were when Brock's phone sounded. It was Carson.

"That was fast, I thought you would be a couple of days." Brock shares his assumption.

"My editor is super excited, and she wants me to have a story to her within a week. Is it possible for me to see the documents?"

"Sure, I've made a few copies. Where can I deliver them?"

Carson responded, "I'm staying up here at the cottage for two more days. I can go to you if you don't want to come out here."

"I'll bring them to you. I'll be there in an hour."

*****

Brock went to the cottage door and stuck his head in. He greeted everyone before looking at Carson, "There are two boxes, do you want them transferred into your car or do you want me to bring them in?"

"I can't wait to see them, so I'll help you bring them in."

Brock stayed and talked with Andrew and Gregory after he made sure he wasn't interrupting anything. Carson had opened the first box and was analyzing the documents. "This evidence is wonderful. I'll draft the story and I would like to add a personal touch so I want to interview your father. If you give me his number, I'll contact him."

He looked at Andrew and Gregory, "I'm too excited to get started so I think I'll head into the city tonight and get going. We're ahead of schedule here so I feel comfortable I can get this story wrapped up in the next couple of days and I'll be ready for our three days of interviews next week."

Gregory pointed to his broken leg, "I'm not going anywhere. See you next week. Good luck!"

Andrew helped Carson out to the car with the boxes and said goodbye before returning to the cottage.

Making A Difference

Brock was getting an update on Gregory's leg when Andrew joined them. He filled them in on the status of the shelter and talked about the work on the pavilion and the surrounding park area was progressing.

They asked him to stay for supper, but he declined, "Thank you but Dirk and I have plans for tonight."

Gregory spoke up, "You two seem to have hit it off really well."

"We have. I wallowed for four years over Matthew, thinking he was coming back. When I met Dirk, the lights came on and I saw the world in a whole different way."

"What wonderful plan do you have for tonight?"

"You know how I've been saying for years that I wanted to remodel Mammie's place but never did anything. Well, when I was showing Dirk around, I mentioned the remodel and he's gung-ho to help. This weekend, we plan to tackle my bedroom. The biggest job is removing all the old wallpaper; it has to be forty years old."

"Good for you! It's said that wallpapering together is a test of any relationship. We've remodelled many an old home, and wallpaper is a challenge whether you're putting it on or taking it off."

*****

The movie credits rolled, and Brock didn't move. He was spooning Dirk, and he didn't want to give up the warmth, so he stayed. He reached for the remote sitting just above his head on the arm of the sofa. The click brought a silence that needed to be broken, "Dirk, you've told me a bit about your life, but I want to know your life from the beginning of your memory to now. Would you be comfortable sharing your story?"

"I'll tell you whatever you want to know but I'm afraid I'll bore you."

"Try me. I want to know your parents, your siblings and anyone important in your life."

They stayed snuggled together and Dirk started his story. He talked about his earliest memory of a fire. He would have been three and his brother had just arrived home from the hospital. They lived in an old house which had faulty wiring and when they plugged a bottle warmer in, it kept blowing fuses, so Dirk's dad put a penny in instead and it got the bottle warmer working, but the overload started a fire. Dirk had been playing in the bedroom with the fuse box in the closet when smoke started pouring into his room. He yelled for his father, and they had to evacuate.

Making A Difference

His memory just had glimpses of that event and he listed what he remembered. Dirk rolled to face Brock, "Am I boring you yet?"

Brock murmured into Dirk's shoulder, "Not at all, keep going."

Dirk spoke about where his parents grew up in New Brunswick and that his grandparents on both sides still lived in those homes. William, his father, was from Grand Falls, and Jean, his mother, was from Red Bank. He talked about his parents meeting through his mother's best friend who happened to be his father's first cousin. It was love at first site and they married and moved to Fredericton where his father was a police officer and his mother an office manager. He had one younger brother, Jack, who lived in Wolfville, Nova Scotia and was doing his PhD in mathematics. He had a part-time teaching position and hoped he could become a professor at Acadia University.

He filled Brock in on his education and how his first app was a success which allowed him to open his own IT firm and employ forty-six people. He talked about his relationship with Douglas and how he went into a severe depression when he died. Then he talked about going to the Pine Valley Garden Centre and meeting a wonderful man. "That brings us up to today and I'm hoping the story will continue onward for many years."

Brock was satisfied with the story and added, "I hope it includes me."

"I hope it does too. Now it's your turn. Piece together your life for me."

Brock gave it some thought, "OK. Once upon a time….."

Chapter 30

Callie sat talking with Mackenzie in her office. She had been visiting on a regular basis since she moved back home. She explained that her parents were still going to Pflag meetings with her, and they have treated her with respect since she moved back in, "I think they're afraid I'll leave again. Of course, I would, if things go bad again, but I think this is the new world for me. I have parents who are willing to learn and adapt to keep me in their lives. It is more than words and it feels really good."

"How is school going?"

Callie thought for a few seconds, "I want to say it's going well and, it is. I like the courses I've chosen but a part of me feels like I'm missing something."

Mackenzie was intrigued, "Can you explain that feeling?"

"I don't know but I'll try. With my life back together, I know the courses are the right ones for right now, but I guess I'm having a difficult time putting it all together. It's like finishing a jigsaw puzzle but there are pieces missing and I can't see the whole picture yet."

"Do you know what you want to do when you're done your studies?"

"I know I want to work helping people, but I'm not sure what that help looks like yet. I see you making a difference with your job, and I see Tom is making a difference with his job so I guess I need to find out what the difference I want to make will be."

"Would you be interested in coming to the shelter and putting on workshops to help the residents determine what they want to do with their lives. I find that when I teach, I learn as well."

"I think I'd like that. Will I have to develop the workshop?"

"I've been looking at workshops that I can purchase, and one is geared to helping people determine what they want to do with their lives. I thought it would be good for the residents. I didn't know who would be facilitating them but if you want to, I can help you get ready for the classroom."

"I've never done anything like this before but if you help, I'll do it. When will the workshops be here?"

Mackenzie liked her eagerness, "I'll place the order today and I'll let you know when they arrive.

Making A Difference

*****

Carson spread the contents of the box on the floor and then sorted the documents into piles. He then summarized at a high level what he had to work with. He organized his thoughts and came up with an approach. Brock told him about his father having been abused by the priest and suggested he could make it about him starting the class-action lawsuit. That would allow other victims to know someone was publicly acknowledging being abused. He called the number Brock had given him. When Grant answered, he explained who he was and that he wanted to interview him.

Grant was happy to hear this, "I want this to happen as I welcome this interview as soon as you can do it."

Carson was encouraged, "How about today. I'm flexible, so you choose the time."

"I'm home right now so if you could get here soon, I'll wait for you." He gave Carson his address.

"I'll be there in ten minutes. See you soon."

Carson was true to his word and arrived exactly ten minutes later. Martha greeted him and he followed her into the living room where Grant was seated. She brought refreshments and sat to listen to the interview.

Carson wanted to know Grant's story, "I'd like to hear about the abuse and we'll talk about what you're comfortable having in the article."

Grant offered, "I'll tell you my complete story and then we can discuss what you think you need to include. Remember, the purpose of your article is to encourage other victims to come forward."

Carson was elated, "I'll record your story if that's OK."

Grant agreed and started telling how he became a victim of abuse. He talked about how Father Mike built their special relationship and stepped through the timeline of how the meetings in the First-Aid room started out innocently and progressed into pleasurable sex. He relived the day he and the bishop opened the door to find Father Mike with another altar boy and how that felt. He explained his therapy sessions where he struggled to call it abuse but was able to concede that an adult should not take advantage of a child.

Carson asked questions for clarity as the story unfolded and when Grant was finished, Carson felt he had the angle he needed to make this article do the work of bringing more victims forward. He thanked Martha and Grant and went back to his place and wrote. He worked all through the night and when he awoke after only four hours sleep, he knew he had one more aspect he needed to include. He sent it off to his editor and within the hour he got the revised article. The editor had changed very little and was ready to publish. The article would be in the next week's edition of the newspaper.

*****

When Mackenzie walked into the shelter, Tom came up to her carrying a package. "This arrived for you. I think it's the workshop you ordered for Callie."

Mackenzie took the package into her office and opened it while Tom watched, "This is it. I want to review it to make sure this is something Callie will be able to be successful with. I don't want to set her up for failure."

Tom offered, "I have a few hours this morning and I'd love to look it over. I've been interested since you told me about your plan."

Mackenzie liked his exuberance, "I won't have time until after lunch but I'd like to know how you feel about it."

They met after lunch and Tom gave the pros and cons of the workshop. The pros were very good, and the few cons could be easily adjusted with a little work. "I really like the material; it's well developed and easy to understand. The exercises could go awry if guidance isn't given so that's where the facilitator can make a difference. I think people will be able to leave this workshop with a better understanding of what they want to do with their lives."

"Thanks Tom. I'm hoping Callie will be able to learn about herself as she facilitates the workshop. I'll call and help her get ready."

Mackenzie called Callie and told her the workshop was in. Callie was available to go to the shelter right away so Mackenzie told her to come along, and she would get the conference room ready so they could lay the materials out. She asked if Tom could join them, and Callie agreed.

They went through each of the modules in detail. Tom explained the intent of each and how the exercises moved participants to examine themselves from different perspectives. They talked at length about each of the deliverables from the workshop. As they talked, Callie's observations and questions showed she was skilled with analytical insight. By the end of the day, Callie felt she would be able to facilitate the workshop and they booked the date a month away for her first one.

Making A Difference

Mackenzie explained how she would advertise the workshop and offered Callie any help she needed to get ready.

*****

Gregory was getting, what he called *'cabin fever'* and needed to get out of his chair and out of the cottage. They decided to visit Pine Valley Garden Centre and pick up a few plants to fill in a couple of places in the garden, but their main reason was to get Gregory out.

Using his crutches, Gregory manoeuvred around the garden center making sure not to put any weight on his injured leg while he would stop to look at something. A couple of times, he sat to rest but, for the most part, he stayed moving. While they were admiring some of the holly bushes that were on sale, they spotted Brock coming towards them.

Brock greeted them and looked down at the therapeutic boot Gregory was wearing, "I see you have progressed from the initial cast. You're clearly on the mend."

Gregory nodded, "Yes, I love this walking boot! With the cast, I had to wrap it in plastic and prop it on a low stool in the tub so I could sit in about three inches of water. With this boot, I can take it off and get in the tub full of water. I'll never again take for granted the ability to enjoy a long hot soak in a tub. It's pure heaven!"

Andrew waited for Gregory to get his point out and he switched topics, "Brock, I hear you have started work on Pine Valley's pavilion, art gallery, botanical gardens and the arboretum. You must be pleased."

Brock took a deep breath and exhaled slowly, "I'm pleased but sometimes I wonder if I've taken on too much. I know Dad could do this whole project without me, but I have a hard time staying away. I guess I'm too nosey."

Andrew laughed, "We would be the same. We have always needed to be on site every day when we've gotten things done. We've probably gotten in the way of the work when we show up, but no one kicked us off."

Brock remembered they were here looking at plants. "Are you looking for anything special?"

"Gregory wanted to get out of the cottage, so we came here. We always love looking around garden centres. We find it a great way to kill time. How are you and Dirk doing, have you started the remodelling yet?"

Making A Difference

"We're still on course to start on Saturday. There's a part of me that doesn't want to do it because I'm erasing another piece of Mammie." Brock looked a bit sad.

Andrew looked at Brock and soothed, "You can never erase Mammie from your life, she's part of you, and you carry her with you in everything you do. She wouldn't want you to live with her old, outdated wallpaper, my God, it has to be an antique by now and not a good antique. You have to admit it's ugly." He poked Brock and made him smile.

"You're right. I need to put that sentiment aside and make her place mine like she wanted me to do."

Gregory added, "Think of how wonderful your home will be with paint replacing all of the wallpaper. I think you told us Mammie had lamented to you that she would have changed it but she was just too old to bother. She knew you were getting the house and you needed to decorate it according to your personality. Remember they are all things. Like Andrew says, your memories will keep her a part of your life until you die."

"Thanks for the support, I seem to need it." He gave them a discount card for their purchases. "Present this when you check out and they should give you this discount. I've got to run and check out what's happening at the pavilion site. See you later!"

Andrew and Gregory responded in unison. "Thanks Brock! See you later."

Making A Difference

Chapter 31

Brock and Dirk were dressed in their oldest work clothes to tackle the first phase of the remodel, stripping all the old wallpaper off each of the rooms. After discussing the work, they formulated a planned approach which had them start with the master bedroom. They cleared the furniture out and stood looking at the walls covered in large roses from the 1980s.

Dirk let out a prolonged low whistle and said, "Man, this is ugly. I'm so used to modern clean lines and now I know why!"

Brock laughed and faux punched his arm, "Don't judge Mammie's decorating taste in front of me; you could hurt my feelings!"

"I'm not out to say anything bad about Mammie, but you kept this hideous wallpaper on for, what's it now, almost eight years. That I could say something about."

"Life got in the way, so I plead guilty, but I'm so glad you're here with me to help correct my inability to act on such an eyesore." Brock said with determination.

They had several tools and they tried each of them until they found what worked best. By lunch they had the large wall, behind where the bed was, done. They went to the kitchen for something to eat. Brock had prepared the ingredients for submarine sandwiches and they each selected what they wanted and made their lunch. They sat at the dining table and took their first rest of the day while in between biting and chewing, they talked.

"You love this old house, don't you?" Dirk asked.

"I do. I can feel Mammie's presence here and that, alone, is enough to make even the most somber day, a happy one for me. I wish you could have met her. I know she would have liked you." Brock's eyes watered as he spoke.

Dirk saw his reaction and said, "I was hoping we could move in together and my home has my office in it so I thought you might move in with me. Now, I'm wondering if you would ever consider leaving here?"

Brock's surprise was evident, "You want to move in together?"

"I was hoping. You spend most of the time we're together at my place, and we hardly ever come here. I think we get along really well, and I love having you with me, especially when you go to sleep and wake up beside me." Dirk stopped short realizing he was pleading his case and he wanted Brock to want to move in without feeling he was being pressured.

"Dirk, I love you and although it would be difficult to consider moving out of here, nothing would stop me from being with you. Mammie, by the way, was a very wise soul and she would be the first one to kick my butt if I didn't move in with you!"

"I love her already! So, will you move in with me into our home?"

"I spend almost all of my time there already. All I need to do is move my personal effects over. One thing I need is to be able to decorate our Christmas tree using Mammie's ornaments. Over the past eight years they have become very special to me. Are you OK with that?"

"As long as I can incorporate my family ornaments into the mix." Dirk looked directly at Brock and waited.

"I like that. We can have our tree represent each of our memories. You and Douglas must have some special ornaments and they need to be there as well." Brock smiled.

Dirk went to Brock and embraced him, "Thank you for including Douglas. I love you more for that."

"He was an important part of your life, and I wouldn't have it any other way." They kissed. "Let's get back to work. I secretly set our goal to get the whole room done before we leave here."

"Thanks for telling me that now! Let's go get it done!"

They were all set up so getting the two smaller walls done by mid afternoon was easy, but the second larger wall loomed over their goal. While they worked, Brock decided to share information about his father's court case. He hadn't told him, but Carson's story was due out soon and it would be out to the world. Dirk listened intently as he worked and asked a few questions about how his father was dealing with the abuse. Brock started his story when his father was an altar boy and brought him up to present. Dirk asked questions to help him understand the situation. When he heard about the Carson's story being in the paper the coming week, he said he would look forward to reading it and hearing about the response they got from other victims.

They grabbed a quick snack and a cold drink and in under five minutes they were back at work. As they stripped off the last piece, they could hear the Trinity Anglican Church bell sound the hour. They each got out their phones to check the time, five o'clock on the nose!

Brock high-fived Dirk, "We did it!" and zeroed in for a kiss.

Making A Difference

"Dare I ask what other secret goals you've set?" Dirk looks skeptical.

"I haven't set any rigid goals, but I was hoping we could have all of the wallpaper in the house off by the end of the month. The living room, dining room, hallway, and second bedroom will require four or five workdays like today, so I think that's doable. Can we start work on the living room tomorrow?"

"I set tomorrow aside because I didn't think we would finish in here in one day so sure, let's do it. Before we leave here today, we could clear out the artwork and some of the smaller furniture. What about putting the house back together, what's your plan?"

"I've hired a professional who will skim coat the plaster walls to make them smooth and then paint them. She asked me to let her know when the first room was ready so she could use it as a filler between jobs. She will work weekends so maybe she'll work here tomorrow." Brock got his phone out, searched for a number and called. He hung up saying, "She'll be here at nine o'clock. I must get primer and paint. We can do that when we leave here and bring it with us tomorrow."

Dirk calculated their timeline, "Well, we had better get the things out of the living room and go to Home Hardware."

*****

They worked hard on Sunday and were able to get the living room stripped by mid afternoon They stood back.

"Is it just me or was this easier than the bedroom?" Dirk suggested.

Brock looked around, "I was thinking that exact thought earlier and did some mental calculations. Even though this is a larger room, the spaces of wall taken up by the two wide archways and the large picture window result in fewer wallpapered surfaces."

"Well, I, for one, am glad. I'm so sore from yesterday I tortured my body today, so I'm not looking forward to tomorrow. At least I'll be sitting in my office most of the day. How's the painter doing?"

"Let's go look." They walked to the bedroom and Amber, the painter, had just finished rolling the last wall and was cleaning up. "The ceilings and walls are done, and I'll be leaving after I clean my tools. Tomorrow, I'll paint all the trim."

Brock took a key from his pocket. "Amber, here is a key to the back door. Please come and go as you need to, to get your work done. We're finished with the living room so you can start painting there when you're ready. The paint is labeled in that pile."

Making A Difference

Amber looked the paint over and responded, "Great, you have it for all the rooms. I think I'll be fine. You say you won't be able to get at the rest of the wallpaper until next weekend. I've had a cancellation so if you would like me to finish the stripping, I could do that and then paint all the rooms."

Brock was thrilled, "If you could do that, I'd love it. Just let me know what I owe you."

Dirk joined in, "You have made my week. I was dreading coming back next Saturday. Thank you!"

"We'll leave you to clean your tools." Brock looked at Dirk, "We need to clean up and go to supper. Thank goodness it's only next door!"

They went to the bathroom with their change of clothes and began shaving at the one sink and mirror. Dirk, weaving back and forth trying to shave at the same time as Brock said, "I'm glad I have double sinks at my place."

Brock heard the back door close, so he knew Amber had left. "I couldn't help but notice you're back to *'my'* place. You called it our place when you asked me to move in."

"When you have your personal effects there, it will officially be our place. I need to keep something to motivate you!" He laughed as he stepped into the shower as Brock finished at the sink.

Brock joined Dirk under the hot shower and embraced him from behind. He nuzzled the soft hollow in his neck and he almost swooned. Dirk turned to face him, and Brock saw and felt that the nuzzle worked its magic. They spent several minutes taking care of each other's needs before turning the water off. They were towelling off when Brock leaned in and kissed him softly on the lips, "I love you, Dirk."

They dressed and walked over to Brock's parents' house. Mackenzie and Tom were there.

She gave him a raised-eyebrow look, "We stopped in to pick you up but all we could hear was the shower and you didn't answer our 'hello' so we left. You might want to lock your door when you're not able to answer it."

Brock blushed, "Amber, our painter, left after we went to clean up so we couldn't lock the door." He needed to steer the conversation elsewhere, "How are things at the shelter?" She winked at him letting him know she knew what he was doing, "It's a good thing we did the expansion because we continue to have very low vacancy if any."

They sat down for supper and table conversation centred around the lawsuit and their chances to win.

Making A Difference

Dirk looked to Grant, "Brock explained your lawsuit to me, and I just want to tell you I admire what you're doing. Thank you for the difference you'll be making in so many people's lives. My father was also an altar boy and became a victim of a priest. He carries that pain to this day. So much so, he removed himself from the Catholic religion and we were brought up in Mom's United Church of Canada."

Brock looked at Dirk, "You didn't mention that to me."

Dirk responded, "Sorry, I should have. I've lived my life by not being allowed to talk about it and it's still difficult to do. This moment felt right."

Grant felt he could help, "Would he be interested in joining the lawsuit?"

"I can ask, but he hasn't processed the abuse like you have so I'm not sure how he'll feel. I'll let you know."

"I'd be willing to talk with him if he needs someone to talk to. It can be quite lonely when you feel there isn't anyone who would understand. When did he tell you about the abuse?"

Everyone was enthralled with this conversation. Dirk continued, "He never did. One night he came home drunk, and he was spouting off at Mom while sitting in the kitchen. I happened to be just in the hallway and heard what he was saying. I spoke with Mom after Dad went to bed and she filled in the blanks. Alcohol is what he chose to help him cope and he gets drunk, not every day but often. He isn't a mean drunk, but he does get sad and frustrated. Since I learned of his abuse, I have a better understanding of why."

"

Chapter 32

The lawyer called a special meeting for Friday afternoon and Grant arrived with his family in tow. Axel had an excited and nervous energy they hadn't seen in their previous meetings. It seemed he couldn't sit down, and he paced the floor. When the Mathesons found their place around the conference table, he started, "Your reporter did a better job than I could ever have expected. His newspaper story has hit nerves. It was printed on Tuesday and by Wednesday it had been picked up by newspapers across the country. Victims started signing on to a special website our firm developed to capture their details and so far, we have 237 people who want to join your class action suit. This bodes well for our chance of success. We've hired several people to call each of the victims and get their details. We'll cross reference that information with Father O'Hara's documentation and see if they fit. If they do, they are in for sure but if they don't, we'll have to see how we can represent them. They were still abused, so we need to determine how we can handle them. I think we're building a strong case so they might be able to ride on the coattails of our documentation and still be heard even though we do not have any supportive documentation for them….yet."

Grant caught Axel's excitement, "So, when victims call in, your team processes each one to see if they link to any of the abusers Father Mike documented. That sounds like a lot of work. How soon could this go to court?"

Axel thought for a few long seconds and responded, "Even though victims will be contacting us for weeks, maybe months to come, I think we can launch the suit soon. Staff have been organizing the documentation so we can present a cohesive picture of the church knowing about the abuse and hiding it without much consideration for the victims. We were able to contact Albert, the boy who was being abused when you and the bishop opened the door and caught them. He was reluctant but when we told him you, Grant, were launching a lawsuit, he agreed to come on board. Grant, the church didn't know about you, but they did know about Albert. The fact is, this may not reach trial until next year, but that will give us lots of time to make it as strong as we need to tackle a church with high-paid lawyers who have been through this many times and know their stuff. I need to see if I can get transcripts of some of the suits to see what I need to be able to address in the courtroom. Preparation takes time but pays off in the long term."

Making A Difference

"Is that going to make a difference?" Grant asked.

Axel explained, "It shouldn't, because you have the letter from Father O'Hara confessing to the abuse and he sent you damning documentation of all of his victims as well as those of other priests. We can't peg the church for hiding your relationship with Father Mike, but we can get them on you being abused by a priest, so you still fit. The priest hid you, not the church's hierarchy."

"Is there anything we need to do?" Martha asked.

Axel shook his head, "No, you have done everything you can do so if something comes up, I'll let you know. As the trial date gets closer, we can add victims to the suit as we verify their information. That's only something we can do, unless someone approaches you on their own and doesn't fill their information out on the website. If that happens, we need them documented, so convince them to contact us."

*****

Grant ended his call and Martha heard only enough of it to heighten her interest, "Was that the lawyer?"

"Yes, The Catholic Church is upset we released the story. They are accusing us of slander, so their lawyers have asked us to cease and desist or they'll counter sue."

Martha looked frightened, "What does Axel think we should do?"

"He says this is a normal tactic lawyers use to scare the complainant into submission. They don't know what evidence we have so they're running scared and will do whatever they can to get us to drop the suit."

"So, what does he recommend?"

"Stay the course and document all of the victims. For each person who contacts us they capture the name, address, phone numbers, and email address. They then document who the abuser was, where and when the abuse happened, who knew about it, and what the Church did about it. With this documentation, they try to connect the victim to any of the abusers Father Mike documented. If they can, it's corroborated evidence. If we can't, they still keep the data on the victim and they'll be part of the suit, just not with the solid evidence we have for those who coincide with the information we have."

"So, that was an update call."

"He needed to tell me because the Church's lawyers may seek me out because I was front and centre in Carson's article. He says they may try to intimidate me. All I have to say is, bring it on!"

Making A Difference

*****

Brock and Dirk met uptown by chance and decided to go see how Amber, the painter, was doing. Dirk had just finished with his lawyer and Brock was in town to do a cash deposit for the garden centre. Brock had taken clothes for the week and stayed at Dirk's place, so he hadn't seen the progress.

When they walked into the living room and dining area, they were dumbfounded. The walls were pristine. Amber had skim coated and painted the walls and it looked like a new house. The hallway in the foyer was finished as well and they walked into the bedroom hallway which was also done. They heard a noise in the second bedroom and Amber was just applying the final coat of paint.

Brock greeted Amber and looked around, "You have done an amazing job, I never expected you would have this all done so fast! I'm so happy with the new look."

Amber loved happy clients, "I'm glad you like it. I'll be finished today, unless there's other work you want me to do."

Brock thought, "That's all of the wallpaper, but the kitchen and bathroom could use a fresh coat of paint. Do you have time to do the ceilings, walls, and trim like the other rooms you did?"

"I can squeeze them in, they're not big jobs but I'll need paint. I'd like to start tomorrow. Does this work?"

Brock looked to Dirk, "I guess we're going to buy paint. I need to stop at Mom and Dad's first though. Amber, thanks so much. I'll have the paint here so you can start tomorrow. See you later."

They left there and walked up to Brock's parents' home and went in.

They had planned a simple supper for later so they could spend a few minutes.

They greeted each other and hugged all around. Brock explained how great his house looked and went on and on about the job Amber was doing.

Martha was excited, "I need to go over and see it. Can we go now?"

Brock mentally calculated his time, "Can we do it another day? That way the whole house will be done. Tell you what, I'll get the house set up and we'll have you and Dad over for supper and do a grand reveal. Amber should be done by the day after tomorrow so let's do Friday."

Making A Difference

"Sounds like a date! Since you're here, stay for supper. My chicken pot pie will be ready in five minutes, and I made rolls too. Will you stay?"

Dirk spoke up, "I don't know about him," pointing to Brock, "but I will!" Everyone laughed and went about setting the kitchen table.

As they ate, they talked about what was going on in their lives. Grant told them about the call and said he was going to continue, "I don't intend to stop when I've gone this far."

Dirk added, "Martha, I have to say this chicken pot pie rivals my mom's version and the rolls are amazing."

"Thank you. I am glad you like them." Martha was pleased.

"I called home after the last Sunday supper, and I told Mom about the lawsuit. She had seen the article, so she was surprised that I was kind of connected. She said Dad had read the article but said nothing. She's going to mention it to him. I'll let you know when I hear from her."

"Great, when you spoke to your mom, I hope you mentioned I'd be open to talking with your dad."

"Our family hasn't talked about this so I've asked Mom to see if she could open it up so we could talk about it but she is hesitant, so we'll see. With her so nervous, I forgot to mention it but I will."

They finished the meal, but Martha surprised them, "We have dessert."

Grant went to the kitchen to help with dessert plates and forks while Martha got the pie, a knife, and a pie server.

As Martha walked in, she announced, "I hope everyone likes blueberry pie and ice cream."

Dirk laughed, "You obviously mean me because you know the rest of the room does. I love blueberry pie, especially with vanilla ice cream!"

They ate almost too much. Brock and Dirk thanked them and excused themselves so they could get to Home Hardware before it closed. "I need to leave paint for Amber for tomorrow morning." They shared hugs all around before they left.

*****

Dirk called his mother the next morning. She was surprised, "Honey, is something wrong?"

"No Mom, the other night we talked about the lawsuit, and I was wondering if you spoke to Dad."

Making A Difference

"I'm easing into it with him so, a bit at a time. I'll let you know how I make out."

"I forgot to tell you that Brock's father, Grant Matheson, has offered to talk with Dad. He says he found it helpful to talk to someone who won't judge. I don't know all of the details with Dad's abuse, but Grant is easy to talk to and will not judge because he's been through it himself. He's the one the article is written about. He wants to help people get out from under all the shame and guilt."

"I'll talk with him. How is everything else? Are you and Brock getting along well?"

"We're getting along so well. Unless he's hiding something, he's the one. I never thought I'd find someone after Douglas died but I think I have."

"Oh Honey, I worried about you and now this takes a load off my mind. I was almost ready to drive down for a visit to see how you are."

"Mom, why don't you and Dad come anyway?"

"That's a great idea. Dad and I have a bit of time set aside; I'll let you know when. I love you!"

"Love you too!" He hung up the phone and entertained the idea of the visit. Why hadn't he thought about that?

*****

Mackenzie, Tom, Dirk, and Brock arrived at Andrew and Gregory's cottage and Tom was introduced. They sat in the living room and munched on appetizers while they summarized important news in each of their lives. Andrew and Gregory talked about Gregory's accident and how his healing was doing, and they heard about Tom's family in Truro, and Dirk's family in Fredericton. Tom and Dirk sat and listened to the stories all four had about their collective times in *'the manor'* and laughter filled the air.

Andrew went to the kitchen and Brock followed. As they were getting things organized, Brock lowered his voice, "Andrew, Mackenzie and I are looking for people or organizations needing some help. Our philanthropy is moving into a bigger, more visible entity and we were wondering if you hear of a need, could you send it our way? We still want no one to know about my involvement but we want to formalize a charitable organization with a board of directors beyond Mackenzie and me. We were hoping you and Gregory might be interested."

"I don't even have to check; I know he will go on the board if I do. We've been looking for something like this. Count us in!"

Making A Difference

"Great I'll let you know when we have our next board meeting. In the meantime, keep your ears open for anyone in need."

Chapter 33

Callie burst into Mackenzie's office, "I'm getting so nervous; what if I bomb?" Callie's face was rigid with fright as she looked at Mackenzie.

"That's a natural reaction when you do something for the first time, especially when you're in front of a classroom of strangers. Sometimes it's helpful if you teach a group of people you know, as a test run." Mackenzie suggested. "What do you think of that?"

"Thanks, but I think I might be more nervous with them. I'm going to risk the strangers. I know my stuff, but I always get nervous so, don't worry, I'll get over it."

"Are you saying you're all ready for Friday?"

"I am. I'd like us to sit down some day this week and run over some of the material I have questions about. When are you free?"

Mackenzie looked at her calendar, "I have an hour right now or there's a two-hour slot right after lunch. How much time do you need?"

"I really know the material, so I won't need much time. If we could take the hour now, that would work for me."

"OK, I just need to make a call. We'll use the conference room so get ready with your questions and I'll be in after my call." Mackenzie scanned her notes and picked up her phone.

Callie was well organized and had her questions identified by bright pink pieces of paper sticking out of her Facilitator's Manual. They went through each and Mackenzie found that, in general, Callie was overthinking the material. When they finished, Mackenzie summarized. "You know your material and your questions were at a depth you probably won't get from the students in your class. Remember, I'll be at the back of the room, so you can call on me as a consultant if you need help."

"Thank you. The workshop starts at nine on Friday so I'll be here at eight to set up. How many participants are there?"

"I expect you'll have ten for sure. I do have twelve people registered but I'm not sure about two of them."

"Great, see you on Friday!"

*****

Making A Difference

Brock met Amber at the house, and she went over all the work she had done. He was more than pleased and when he paid her, he gave a hundred-dollar tip.

"She counted it out and remarked, "Here's an extra hundred. You paid me too much."

"I appreciate what you've done so that's a tip for the quality of work, your professionalism, and excellent customer service. Thank you!"

Amber left and Brock was about to go back to the garden centre when his mom walked in the back door, "I saw you arrive so I thought it would be a good time to have a look at the house." As she walked from room to room, she exclaimed, "It looks so different, it's hard to tell it's the same place. It strikes me as being much more modern than I know it is. Everything looks so spacious. Great job, Brock!"

"It is and now I'm in a dilemma. We spend all of our time at Dirk's place, and he has a special office area where he runs his business. It's a natural next step that we move in together and it makes sense we live there. My dilemma is, I don't want to sell Mammie's place."

Martha offered, "Could you rent it when the time comes? If you can get a good tenant who will look after the place, you'll still have it should you need it in the future."

Brock pondered her suggestion, "I wouldn't want just anyone. Maybe Matthew and Neal would move in? I hear they have a place, but I could wait until their lease is up if they want it."

"Matthew would be a great tenant. It sounds like you solved your dilemma."

"I'm in no rush but I'll approach him."

*****

Gregory was working with Blair, his physio therapist, doing weight training with his leg. He got Gregory to walk through an obstacle course using his crutches and he found he was getting stronger and stronger as the days went by. When the session was done that day, Blair said, "You're doing well, and it's easy to see you're strengthening your muscles. Tomorrow, I want you to bring your other sneaker and you'll be walking without the boot on a treadmill."

Gregory couldn't believe what he heard, "No offence but how do you know I'm ready for this?"

Blair smiled, "This isn't my first rodeo. I looked at your latest x-rays and you're ready to start putting weight on it in your sneakers. Trust me, I'd do nothing to compromise your healing."

Making A Difference

The next day, Gregory had his boot off and was walking on the treadmill with both feet in sneakers. When he first stood up, he was waiting for pain to shoot up his leg but there was no pain, only an apprehensiveness that he created himself. He realized he was putting weight on his foot for the first time since the accident and he walked a slow pace, but he walked. Blair congratulated him and told him he would build strength over the next sessions until he wouldn't need the boot and could walk comfortably without crutches.

Gregory left there knowing he would be healed enough to be able to help Andrew with the catering at Kaleisha's wedding.

*****

Mackenzie went into the conference room and saw Callie was ready to start. Mackenzie greeted her, "I don't even have to ask if you're ready. Now all we need is someone to teach. I expect to see some of your students soon. Four of them are residents here and I think they need to hear what this workshop is about."

Callie smiled, "I really appreciate all you've done for me, and I'm looking forward to see how I do today."

They chatted for a few minutes when students started arriving. Callie passed around the roster and had each person sign their name. Pretty soon all twelve seats were full, and Callie announced that everyone was there and started the workshop. Callie noticed her nervousness subsided as people introduced themselves. As part of the introduction, she added something funny that happened to them recently. As the people shared, laughter erupted at the funny snippets each person shared and that laughter was what she needed.

As she went from the teaching modules to the exercises, Callie was able to have everyone engaged and was able to answer the questions that were asked. By the time the break arrived, Callie couldn't believe they had used ninety minutes already. As the students had a bathroom break and chatted with the other students, she checked in with Mackenzie.

Mackenzie opened with, "How do you think you're doing?"

Callie shrugged, "I think it's going well. The students seem to want to be here and participate. It feels good."

"It should, you're facilitating like you have been doing this your whole life. I would never guess this was your first workshop. You're a natural."

The rest of the morning was a success, and they broke for a half hour lunch since the food was supplied. Callie ate with Mackenzie but didn't have much

Making A Difference

time to chat because students came up to her and engaged her in conversation. Mackenzie smiled to let her know this was the way it needed to go. She mouthed, *'We'll talk after class.'*

Mackenzie was impressed with how the workshop was going. The afternoon session was amazing to watch as Callie came alive. The room filled with pertinent conversation, perspectives, and questions to clarify what was taught. Any thought that students wouldn't ask questions for fear of sounding dumb was eliminated and the workshop became a robust interactive learning environment. When Callie announced the workshop was over, she thanked the students for their participation. A few students asked to talk with Callie.

The four students who were residents went up to Mackenzie. Mona spoke first, "I remember when Emily, I mean Callie, was here, I never guessed she could teach. This workshop was great. I think I know what I want to do for a job." The other three nodded and said something similar. Mackenzie felt the workshop was a great addition to the shelter.

The last student left leaving Callie gathering up her materials. Mackenzie walked up to her, "Well, how do you think you did?"

"I feel I did a great job. I saw a bit of the feedback and the scoring was good. I'll know better when I see it all. Do you want to see them?"

"Let's have a look. I can't image anyone having anything negative to say."

They reviewed the forms with serious looks which turned into smiles, and they pointed out to the other something on the form they were reading. When they finished comparing the feedback, Mackenzie said, "You should feel very accomplished with how you did in this workshop. I know I'm proud of you!"

Callie hugged Mackenzie, "Thank you. I think I finally know what I want to be. I want to go into teaching."

"Congratulations on discovering your calling! You'll make a great teacher."

"As I was teaching and the students were engaged, I was thinking you have made a difference in my life, and I was making a difference in the students' lives. Thank you Mackenzie!"

Chapter 34

Bonny, Doug, and Matthew were seated in the waiting room in the Oncology Department with messages going through each of their minds. Dr. Bradley had done testing at six months from his 'all clear' diagnosis and wanted to see them to give them the results. They filed into the room and sat in anticipation of what the tests showed. The door opened and when Dr. Bradley entered, they couldn't tell anything from his demeanor.

"I reviewed your new tests, and the cancer is back and fast growing." Dr. Bradley laid out in the utter silence in the room. Bonny broke down while Doug sat in numb realization. Matthew comforted his mother and encouraged her to hear the doctor out.

Doug snapped out of his numbness and asked, "What does this mean for treatment?"

"We want to do some follow-up testing to determine how big the tumour is and what options we have. Once I have those, we can set a course of treatment. When I got your results, I booked the tests for today." He explained the tests were like the ones Doug had to determine the treatment last time. "I expect to examine the scans and be able to set a course of treatment. I booked you an appointment for this Friday at two o'clock. Can you make that?"

Bonny knew whatever was on the calendar could be moved, "We'll be here."

Matthew decided to stay with his parents so he called Anson to explain the situation and tell him he wouldn't be back in the office until the morning.

The testing was completed, and they drove home in silence. As they drove by a cemetery Doug pointed, "We should get our grave sites."

Bonny was taken back and uttered, "We don't need to be concerning ourselves with that right now, do we?"

"Bonny, I know so many people who receive an all clear and within the year they are dead. I'm thinking that if this is terminal, I will choose MAID." Doug said without emotion.

"What's maid?" Bonny looked puzzled.

"It stands for Medical Assistance in Dying. If this is terminal, I'll choose to end my suffering early and have the doctors give me medication to help me die."

Making A Difference

"You're not being put down like a dog, don't be crazy." Bonny looked to Matthew for his support.

"Mom, if Dad wants that, we can talk about it when we know what the tests show. Before we know that, we're jumping to conclusions. Let's find out what Friday brings and discuss treatment at that time. Will you both agree to this?"

Both his mother and father gave a resigned nod. The rest of the drive home returned to silence.

*****

Matthew arrived at his home and sat on the sofa. He stared at the opposite wall without really knowing he was. He thought about the day at the hospital and try as he might to not guess what Friday would bring, he went down several roads, some good, some not good at all. He came out of his catatonic state when he heard the front door close and Neal shout, "Honey, I'm home." A comic habit they created from a sitcom they watched when they first moved in together.

"In here, Neal."

Neal followed the sound and found Matthew on the couch. "You look beat, what's up?"

"Dad's cancer is back and it's fast growing." He filled him in on what the doctor said, the tests he had arranged, and the appointment for Friday.

Neal went over, hauled Matthew up and embraced him. They stood there for several minutes, and Matthew started sobbing. Neal held him until the tears subsided.

Matthew looked at Neal, "I promised I wouldn't go the gloom and doom route because I need to be there to support my parents. They're taking this worse than I am and look at me, I'm a mess."

"Friday isn't far away so you'll know soon enough. Whenever people hear the word cancer, they think the worst, that's natural. Maybe we'll be standing here this time next week with a new understanding that isn't as grim."

Neal lifted Matthew's chin and kissed him on the lips. At first Matthew didn't feel anything but then there was a spark and he wanted more. Neal could feel him come alive and he kissed his neck and nuzzled his ear. Matthew revelled in the feelings and nothing else filled his head. He took Neal by the hand and led him to their bedroom. Matthew slowly undid the shirt buttons and tongued his nipples ever so lightly. Neal threw his head back to feel the full force of the current flow across his chest and down his torso. He needed Matthew and took charge undoing his buttons replicating Matthew's actions. Matthew savoured the feelings and pressed his body into Neal's. They both felt their swollen cocks touch, setting off a feverish

Making A Difference

need. They helped each other out of their pants and pressed their bodies together thrilling as their cocks slid against the hardness of the other. The need overtook the play, and their briefs found the floor as they fell onto their bed. In an orchestrated exploration only possible by two people who knew what thrilled the other, they relished the smoothness of their skin, rubbed their faces into the coarse reality of each other's chest hair exciting nerve endings, and licked, nipped, and kissed their way to their prize. Their excitement rode the line between pain and pleasure as one then the other released their pent-up desire. They relaxed into an exhausted heap.

Neal leaned into Matthew and breathlessly asked, "Did that take your mind off your worries?"

Matthew smiled, "What worries?"

*****

The days leading up to Friday seemed to pass as if they would never end. Doug had taken to writing notes and hiding them away so no one could see them. Bonny took to baking and the house smelled of delicious opportunities but very little was eaten. She ended up filling the freezer when the baked goods piled up. She couldn't stop herself.

Matthew arrived for lunch, and they chatted about nothing of consequence. No one dared to mention the results which played on each of their minds. They found themselves in the same waiting room seats they were in earlier in the week and they waited. After what seemed like forever, a nurse showed them to the room.

Dr. Bradley came in with Doug's chart, explained the results, and declared there was nothing more they could do except for some palliative chemotherapy and radiation.

Everyone focused on that one word, terminal. Doug was first to speak, "What will the palliative radiation or Chemotherapy do for me? From what I understand you only do five sessions, right?"

"For terminal patients, the palliative treatments are not meant to cure you, but they may shrink the tumours and give you a bit more time to put things in order." Dr. Bradley explained.

Doug digested that, "Do I then just wait for death? How long do I have and how painful will it be?"

Bonny and Matthew sat back and watched the worst-case scenario play out before their eyes. When they looked to each other they both were struggling to stop the tears from breaking free and flow down their faces.

Making A Difference

The doctor explained that the pain would be managed with drugs. As for how long, because the cancer is fast growing, he might have three months at best, but no one could really give an exact date. He suggested they discuss end-care options and offered the Palliative Unit at the hospital, Caring Hearts Hospice, or that he could die at home but cautioned that caregivers are put under a lot of stress.

Doug looked at the doctor, "Can you explain MAID so my wife and son hear the same information I hear."

Dr. Bradley explained that terminal patients could use Medical Assistance in Dying to end their life earlier than through natural processes. "It's done in a painless way with injections and the patient has control over when they would die. Doug is eligible for medical assistance if he chooses it. No one can choose for him, at least as the laws read now."

"I want to talk this over with Bonny and Matthew, so they understand my wishes. I'm not interested in living beyond my awareness. If all I'm doing is breathing while caregivers do my hygiene, I don't call that living. I'll live as long as there is quality in my life, quantity isn't my goal." He looks at his family, "Are there any questions that the doctor can help answer?"

Bonny dried her eyes, "How does it play out? If he said he wanted it, what happens next and who can be with him?"

"It's really quite simple. Doug would tell us he's ready, we set the day two days out and he can have anyone he wants in the room. It can happen anywhere, in a building where they allow it, at home, in nature, wherever Doug would like it to happen. Anything else?" Dr. Bradley waited.

Matthew spoke up, "So, after he passes, he would be treated the same as if he died on his own. As I understand it, he chooses that he wants MAID and sets the date, place, and time. It would be set up and the doctor administers the drugs. Is there anything I'm missing?"

The doctor shook his head, "No, it really is that simple."

"Say I choose MAID and change my mind, can that happen?" Doug wanted Bonny to hear the answer.

"Yes, you can stop it anytime unless the drugs were administered. If you stop it, we do not assist."

"OK, please set it up for me and I'll fill the date in later."

Bonny took in a sharp breath, "Oh, Doug." and started to cry.

"Honey, we'll talk about this at home. I want you to be comfortable with my decision." Doug took Bonny's hand and rubbed it with his other.

Making A Difference

*****

Bonny, Doug, and Matthew chatted about mundane things and stayed away from discussing MAID. It was almost as if they didn't discuss it, it wouldn't happen. Denial at its best.

When they got to the house, Bonny was the dutiful homemaker and brought a selection of baked goods into the living room. Doug selected things he enjoyed, "One thing about dying, I don't have to worry that all these wonderful sweets are going to make me fat or kill me, too late!"

"Doug!" Bonny was aghast at his frivolous comment.

"Honey, we're all dying from the day we come into this world. I just have more information than the rest of you. We take life for granted. Now I'm taking my death for granted and doing whatever I want to do with the rest of the time I have before I pull the plug. Let's discuss how you each feel about MAID."

Matthew went first, "Dad, I've been a proponent for MAID since the government started legalizing it. It makes so much sense that we don't have to suffer the pain and indignity that goes along with dying, especially with a cancer that could cause a slow and painful natural death. You have my vote."

Bonny listened and commented, "What about God? If you get assisted, will you still go to heaven?"

"I think God would understand. Does it matter if I breathe for six more days or whatever and am not aware of what's happening around me to be received into heaven? I think not. I've lived a life loving God and I accept Jesus as my saviour, so I think I have it covered. Remember all the trouble we had reconciling Matthew being gay. I've thought of this situation from several perspectives, and I've come to the realization that God would be OK with this for me."

Bonny nodded, "We had a lot to think about with Matthew being gay and connecting with God. I think God will be OK. If MAID is what you want, I'll support your wish. As we were talking, I realized I'll be mourning you no matter when you die so if you want to eliminate the pain and suffering, I say eliminate it. What do you think of the palliative radiation and chemotherapy?"

"The way I see it is, why would I put myself through the inconvenience and sickness of the treatments so I can live a little more but still be suffering. No, I won't be getting any treatments. I've decided that, with the quality I have right now, we're going to do the things we always wanted to do at least until I can't do them anymore. Let's book our trip to Europe, the one we have talked about for years. We could enjoy two or three weeks before the pain gets to be too much."

"I think that's a great idea. Matthew, would you consider coming with us?"

Making A Difference

Matthew was startled into awareness, "Thank you but this is a trip the two of you should take together. Talk to the doctor and get the drugs that would help Dad. All I need you to promise is that if things get bad, you cut the trip short and fly home."

Doug smiled, "I can agree to that! Bonny, do you want to start the planning so we can go as soon as possible?"

"I'm on it!"

Chapter 35

Kaleisha didn't know if her mom would make it before the storm became the promised blizzard, but the plane landed. She watched as the passengers walked through the gate when she spotted her mom. She walked slower than the others, but she was on her way albeit with her coat wrapped tight around her and the collar up to retain her body warmth. When she walked through the doors, Kaleisha ran to her and wrapped her in a big, long hug swaying back and forth. "Muma, you look frozen!"

"I'm frozen, and my fingers are blue. Look at the snow coming down; how do you ever live here?"

"It took a while, but I became acclimatized, and you would too if you stayed a couple of years." Kaleisha wondered how her mom would get through the next two weeks and how much complaining she would have to listen to.

"I'm not here for a couple of years so that's not going to happen. I hope your home is warm."

After getting her luggage, Kaleisha gave her mother a pair of boots she convinced her to wear them. Muma clomped through the drifting snow with a clumsiness of a newborn calf. They began to giggle at the absurdity of how they must look and laughed all the way to the car.

As they drove to Mahogany Manor, Muma told her about several humourous happenings, and they both erupted into laughter. The stories were interrupted with Muma sucking air in through her teeth every time the car skidded a bit on the accumulating snow. The drive home was an adventure with Muma providing hilarious stories and exaggerated comments about Kaleisha's driving. When they got to the B&B, Roger was shovelling the drift left by the snowplough at the end of the driveway. By the time they parked and got out of the car, their sides were sore from all of their laughing.

Kaleisha hugged Muma again while standing in the snow, and she commented, "I have missed you so much! I haven't laughed like that in years. I think it was on my last visit home five years ago."

Roger put his shovel to the side for later snow clearing and went to meet his future mother-in-law. He held out his hand, but she took the hand and pulled him into a hug; he couldn't believe her strength. They were laughing before she released

Making A Difference

him. He took her luggage in and up to her room while Kaleisha helped her up the stairs to the verandah so she wouldn't fall. The outside was lit up with twinkling lights and colourful decorations but when Muma stepped into the foyer, she stood and took in the scope of the decorations, the like of which she had never personally experienced, "Baby, your place is a Christmas wonderland! It is beautiful!"

Muma spent several minutes wandering through the living room, dining room, and foyer taking in the abundance and beauty. She turned to her daughter, "And this is all yours?"

"It is, Muma. The former owners, Andrew and Gregory, who you'll meet, helped make this happen for me. They have made such a difference in my life and are providing me with support to ensure I don't fail."

"Canada has been very good to you. I always knew you would be a success!"

Kaleisha took Muma for a tour of all the rooms so she could get acquainted with *'the manor'*. They ended the tour in her bedroom and Kaleisha suggested she might want a nap before supper.

Muma made herself at home and before long was greeting the guests and regaling them with stories of her own bed and breakfast in Jamaica. She was the centre of attention and Kaleisha marvelled at how comfortable she was with strangers. As she watched, she became more determined to ask her mom to give her away. The person who would be too shy to do that was certainly not the person she was watching. When her audience moved away, Muma went over to Kaleisha, "What wonderful people!"

Kaleisha saw her chance, "Muma, you seemed to be enjoying yourself with all of the guests and I was wondering if you would be the person to give me away during the ceremony?"

"I definitely will. You're my daughter and it is my responsibility since your late dad can't do it."

*****

The time went quickly, and the wedding day was upon them. Kaleisha's adult children, Alvita and Winston, arrived and Muma went right into grandmother mode.

Kaleisha and Brock were checking lists and made adjustments as needed. The guest list had grown to seventy-three over the weeks and the guys adapted at every addition so there would be enough food. Soon, everything seemed to be in order. The bride and groom as well as Muma and the attendants rehearsed the ceremony by mid-afternoon, and everything was set for the evening wedding.

Making A Difference

Brock managed the set up of the bar and the bartender would arrive by five o'clock. He organized the music that he and Kaleisha had chosen and had a timeline for the special songs she wanted at certain parts of the ceremony. He set up the dining room for the buffet and was only missing the food. He was ready to make this a special night for Kaleisha and Roger. The photographer arrived and had a list of the shots the couple wanted.

Andrew and Gregory had arrived early and had begun preparations for the wedding feast. They surveyed the tables for potential food placement confirming the plans they made with Brock. They knew he wouldn't let them down.

Excitement was growing and the air filled with anticipation and one by one the players went off to get ready. Brock was the first to reappear, looking so handsome in his tux and made the rounds to make sure the decorations and mood lighting were lit around the rooms. The soft glow gave a hyper-romantic mood to the environment. Music wafted through the rooms and greeted people as they arrived. Brock managed the door, took coats, and gave each guest a program for the evening. Dirk took them to the sunroom, asked them to sign the guest book, invited them to enjoy refreshments from the bar, and mingle with the others. Waiters weaved through the growing crowd offering finger foods to stave off any hunger they may have.

Brock was watching the numbers build as time ticked on. There were still ten guests to arrive and only minutes before the ceremony was to start. He asked Dirk to take over while he went to talk to Kaleisha. He explained the situation to her, and she made the decision to give them five minutes and start the music. He communicated the new time to Roger and Winston and returned to Dirk. Six more people had arrived while Brock was away, and he watched the time. At the last minute, the last of the missing guests arrived. They were ready to go. Brock played the music that would tell the groom and best man to descend the stairs in their black tuxes and take their place. Brock started the song Kaleisha had selected for her entrance. Alvita, in a Christmas red velvet dress, appeared on the staircase and took four steps before Muma and Kaleisha, together, walked to the bottom. Muma was in an emerald-green lace dress, and Kaleisha wore a white lace dress with a fitted bodice and wide skirt. The wedding party was the picture of sophistication.

The officiant was efficient and when she asked who would give the bride away, Muna took a step forward and, far from shy, gave a speech about Kaleisha covering her childhood, her father's passing and how he would be so proud if he were there, and ended with how proud she was that her daughter was such a success. No one expected this but everyone clapped when she ended. With a self-satisfied

Making A Difference

smile she stepped back, and the ceremony continued. When the officiant announced them as husband and wife, the room erupted in cheers, applause, and whistles. Kaleisha and Roger kissed, and their subsequent smiles filled their faces with a radiant glow. They signed the necessary paperwork while Andrew, Gregory, Brock, Dirk, Matthew, and Neal helped take the food to the buffet tables. The music changed to background music appropriate for eating and conversation.

After Kaleisha and Roger joined the guests as they partied, she stole a moment to give Brock a hug, "When you described the decorations and said you would duplicate them, I never thought they could be more beautiful than I had imagined. You outdid yourself. Thank you for this wonderful gift."

Brock was proud of his accomplishment and that she loved the decorations, "The best for the best! When you joined us here, you brought something that had never been here before. We were always professional, but you brought life to Mahogany Manor, and I believe that's the main reason the guys chose you to succeed them. Congratulations on your wedding and may you and Roger experience more happiness than even you can imagine. I love you Kaleisha!"

She hugged him again, "Thank you! I love you too, Brock!"

"Hey, hey, hey. What are you doing saying I love you to anyone but me?" Roger joked.

"I love you the most, but I do love others. Get over yourself." She bumped him with her hip and laughed.

"Well, my wife, will you have the next dance with me?"

"I will."

Brock was on cue and hit play for the song Kaleisha wanted as the song that was playing wound down. The dance had started. After the bride and groom, others started to fill the floor and swayed, bopped, and grooved to the music.

The food was disappearing at an alarming rate and the guys were starting to get worried. As they refilled platters, the guests slowed down stuffing themselves and didn't deplete any one variety of food. They rolled the wedding cake out and the cutting ceremony happened without anyone getting cake rammed into their faces, one thing Kaleisha endlessly preached to Roger. They let the guys cut it into pieces which they placed on the buffet table so guests could serve themselves as they desired.

Brock connected with the photographer to check on his progress with the candid shots. He was assured that all the guests had their pictures taken at least twice according to his calculations. Brock smiled, "Kaleisha will be pleased."

Making A Difference

The party ramped up and even Muma commanded the dance floor selecting men at random to dance with her to whatever music that played. She especially enjoyed the calypso music and made it known she had won awards back in Jamaica for her talent. Again, Kaleisha shook her head in disbelief as she witnessed sides to her eighty-three-year-old mother she had never seen before.

Guests started to filter out just after midnight and by one o'clock the rooms were empty except for the main orchestrators of the event.

Kaleisha thanked each of them and gave hugs all round. "Now, Roger and I want each of you to congratulate yourself on making this a very special event. Poor Roger had to listen to me go on and on about this wedding that I think he would probably have preferred to elope, but he stuck with me and my dreams. This wedding has surpassed all my expectations! From the bottom of our hearts, we love you!"

Making A Difference

Chapter 36

Bonny and Doug stood in line to board the tour bus for Paris, one of their top three destinations of their trip. They had spent three days in each of Scotland, Ireland and England having spent the two previous days in London, the first of their top three destinations and today they would be in the second. They boarded the bus, stowed their hand luggage in the overhead compartment and took their seats with Doug at the window so he could experience the scenery. Their schedule suggested having lunch on their own in any of the numerous bistros on the Avenue des Champs-Élysées.

They took the Channel Tunnel to France and arrived in Paris by eleven o'clock in time to check into their hotel before eating. After a briefing and tour maps, they found a bistro and had lunch while they planned out their strategy for the day.

*****

Brock stopped in to see Matthew about a piece of the design for one of the gazebos. They hugged when they greeted each other and went right to work. After finalizing the design, Matthew said he would have it ready in minutes if he wanted to wait.

Brock decided to get an update on Matthew's life, "I hear you and Neal have moved in together. Where are you living?"

"We got a great place on Queen Square South. The building is about 135 years old and the ornate fireplaces, mouldings, and architectural detailing is almost pristine. It has two bedrooms as Neal isn't out to his parents yet and if we have company, we can always bunk together." Matthew winked, "If you get what I mean."

"Dirk and I talked about moving in together and it looks like I'll move into his place because he has the office set up there. His home is amazing, you would love it! I spend most of my time there anyway, so it's almost like I live there already. I don't want to sell Mammie's place, so I'll probably rent it." Brock shrugged his shoulders.

Matthew brightened, "If you did move in with Dirk, would you consider renting Mammie's place to us? I love our place, but it will be expensive to heat over the winter. I took it on impulse when I saw the woodwork without considering the financial aspect of winter. Mammie's will be easier to heat for sure!"

"You would be the perfect tenant! When is your lease up?"

"It's for a year but there is a clause in it that allows us to break it by paying two months rent if the landlord isn't able to find a new tenant right away. It would be worth it for me if we could live at your place." Matthew was vibrating he was so excited.

"Let me talk to Dirk and I'll let you know. I don't want to assume me moving in is a done deal."

"Let me know and we'll give our notice."

"This is perfect. How is your mom and dad?"

Matthew was surprised, "Did you know Dad has terminal cancer?"

"I thought when we talked last spring, he had gotten an 'all clear'. What happened?"

"He did but by his six-month checkup, the cancer had come back. He and Mom are about halfway through a three-week bus tour of Europe right now. They always talked about it and Dad said that while he still had some quality of life, they should do the things they always wanted to until he can't. They're having a great time and it's good to hear the excitement in their voices when they call."

"Your dad is a smart man. So, he's taking it well. How's your mom doing with it?"

"She's hurting but she's being supportive of his wishes."

Brock looked at Matthew, "How are you doing?"

Matthew pursed his lips together like a duck and shook his head, "I really don't know. Some time I break down thinking about what life would be like without him and other times I'm resigned to him doing his death the way he wants. Our relationship has improved so much since I came out to him, so he's like a different person. He's a more compassionate, caring man who seems to finally get me. I spent so much of my childhood avoiding him until I was honest with him about being gay, and he changed. Love has many faces. I'll definitely miss him."

Brock hugged Matthew and stepped back, "I'm so sorry to hear this. If you ever need someone to talk to, I'm your man. You've been a very special person in my life, and I'm glad we aren't avoiding each other anymore. We have both evolved but we were there when we needed each other most. I had hoped we would get back together but after waiting for you for four years, I needed to move on, and then Dirk entered my life."

Making A Difference

"There were many days when I kicked myself for avoiding you, but I really never learned that until I did therapy. Neal came along and I wanted to make you jealous at first but when I saw you with Dirk, I knew my window of opportunity had passed. I then saw Neal for who he is, and I love him so much. He reminds me of you in many ways and in other ways, not so much but it's all good!"

*****

Bonny and Doug spent their last evening in a restaurant in Rome, their third of their top three destinations, reminiscing with the other people on their tour. They had formed some good friendships over the three weeks but never mentioned Doug's terminal cancer diagnosis to anyone. He didn't want to have anyone pity him and Bonny understood.

He had experienced increasing pain over the three weeks. There were small changes which, at first, he ignored but by the end of the first week he had an acute attack of pain that Bonny noticed. They talked about what she saw, and agreed it was time to start taking the medication Dr. Bradley had prescribed before they left Canada. He had developed a potential pain management schedule and explained the pain milestones to them so they would recognize when to start medication or increase the dosage. They incorporated their understanding and Doug's pain was managed well. No one was the wiser.

They flew direct from Rome to Toronto and then caught their flight to Saint John. Matthew met them and helped gather their luggage before taking them home to start working on their jetlag.

As they drove home, they filled Matthew in on the details of their trip that they hadn't given over the phone. They loved seeing how the different countries celebrated Christmas and they spent New Year's Eve in Florence. Matthew particularly liked the excitement with which they shared their stories and thought, *'Mom will have these memories for the rest of her life.'*. By the time they drove into their driveway, everyone agreed the trip had been the right thing to do.

Doug was scheduled for tests the following Monday which were planned before they departed. They would get the results the following Friday.

*****

Dr. Bradley went over the results which showed the rapid growth of the tumour and that the cancer had spread throughout the body. "Your pain management will be critical over the next weeks as the cancer takes over different organs."

With what he heard, Doug needed to know, "Did you arrange for MAID?"

"Yes, it has been arranged and as we get closer, you'll need to select a date and place. I'll be responsible for everything else."

"When the time comes, I would like to go to Caring Hearts Hospice to save my family all the stress associated with home care. Once there, I want you to keep me informed about the progression and we can select the date then." Doug calmly explained.

"I'll support you every step of the way. When you move into Caring Hearts Hospice, the resident doctor will take over your care but I'll be in charge of your MAID so you won't lose me."

*****

By late February, Doug had moved into Hospice. His pain was managed well but he was noticing his energy was diminishing from one day to the next and he found comfort in taking many naps through the day and evening.

One evening Bonny wasn't feeling well and stayed home. With Matthew all to himself, Doug told him that his writing is illegible and asked if he would write down what he said. "I want to write a letter to your mom. Are you OK with that? If not, I can get one of the volunteers to do it instead."

At first Matthew didn't know if he could do it but he reasoned if his father wanted it, he could, at least, do this for him. "Sure, Dad, I'll type it on my iPad as you dictate."

My Darling Bonny,

Sometimes words alone are not adequate enough to express the love I feel but I will try. The strength of my love for you has been a cornerstone for me and helped me through some of the biggest challenges that life threw at us.

We met as kids and married young but growing up together is something I wouldn't trade for anything. You have always been my strength. There were times when I felt I couldn't go on but you convinced me we could and together we worked through them and came out the other side a better couple.

You gave us a beautiful son and as hard as we tried to give him a brother or sister, it wasn't meant to be. God knew we had the best and didn't want any other child to feel inferior.

Our time together will soon come to an end. Just because I stop living doesn't mean you have to stop living. I want you to enjoy life to the fullest. Find someone to share your life. You are a beautiful vibrant woman who deserves love, and you could make some lucky person as happy as you have made me.

I leave this earth with a strong belief in God and I have faith that someday we'll be together again.

All my love,
Doug'

Matthew wiped his eyes, "Dad that's a beautiful and freeing letter. You have given her permission to love again. Thank you!"

"You have my permission to use this letter to encourage your mother to live life to the fullest. I know so many couples who never talked about this and I've seen the surviving partner do nothing because they think they are dishonouring the dead spouse. To me that's hogwash. Let her have some time to mourn if she needs it but don't let her wallow in her grief."

"Don't worry Dad. I'll do whatever I need to do to get Mom to live life again."

"I think I need to sleep. You go spend time with Neal, he must be missing you. I love you Son."

"I love you too Dad."

Chapter 37

Bonny and Matthew walked into Doug's room, as he was signing papers. Bonny asked, "Are those the MAID forms?" She almost didn't ask because she was afraid of what his answer was going to be.

"No, they've already been filled out. Over the past week when I was lying here, I thought about life and death and realized that, although the cancer has destroyed some of my body, other parts of me are just fine so I asked the doctor here if I could donate some of my organs. He told me I have many good parts I could donate so I filled out donor forms and now I'll be able to make a difference in someone's life and in the lives of the people they love. I'm not going out of this world without doing what I can."

Matthew was surprised, "I didn't know you had ever considered organ donation."

"I never did until the thought came to me a week ago. The more I thought about it, the more it made sense. In a way, parts of me will live on through others."

Bonny smiled at Doug, "You have spent your life helping others and now in death you'll continue helping. That is so you!" He looked alive and had colour in his cheeks, more alive than he has looked in weeks. "How are you feeling, you look good."

Doug nodded, "Thank you, I feel good. They put me on a different medication, and it's reduced my pain so I can barely feel it. It does make me tired though, but you've come at the perfect time. I napped for four hours before the doctor brought me the forms to sign. I'd like to go into the common room and look out the window. I'd love to go outside but I don't think I could take the cold."

They got the PSW to get Doug out of bed and into a wheelchair and they wheeled him into the common room. The midday sun was streaming through the glass and Doug closed his eyes against the brightness and soaked up the heat. Bonny and Matthew watched as a peace transcended his face and the smile radiated a feeling that all is right with the world. After several minutes of silence, Doug asked, "You know, if I wasn't going to be able to donate anything, I was going to donate my body to Dalhousie University for their medical program."

"You never talked about that before either. You're full of surprises." Bonny responded.

Making A Difference

"I think having death so close, I'm considering lots of things I let pass by. I want to do the best I can do with the time I have left."

They sat there for two hours, and Doug seemed to enjoy the sun. The room became busy with other residents and their families and Doug decide he wanted to go back to his room. They wheeled him by the nurses' desk and asked for the PSW to put him back in bed.

Once he was settled, they chatted about what was going on out in the community and in their lives. As they talked, Doug's eyes drooped, then closed, and his head lolled to one side.

Bonny whispered to Matthew, "I think we can go and let him sleep."

*****

Matthew was resting in his living room when the doorbell rang. When he opened it, Brock and Dirk were standing there with a bouquet of flowers. He welcomed them in, and they were taking their coats off just as Neal arrived to see what the commotion was. He had been making a spaghetti sauce and his apron showed the earmark of his labours. He explained the mess he was wearing and asked them if they wanted to stay for supper.

Brock spoke first, "We don't want to be a bother. We just wanted to spread a bit of sunshine in your lives. I know what it's like to spend time at Caring Hearts, and I thought these flowers would cheer you up a little."

Neal took over, "You're no bother at all. I'll go put these in water. Supper is about 20 minutes away; would you like something to drink while we wait, water, wine or whatever?"

Dirk offered, "Let me help you so Matthew and Brock can catch up. I want wine, anyone else?" All heads nodded. "Wine it will be."

Dirk followed Neal to the kitchen which showed signs of the cooking Neal was doing and said, "You look after that, and I can pour the wine." Neal had water boiling and he slid the spaghetti into it while he pointed Dirk to the glasses and the wine.

Dirk took drinks to Brock and Matthew and went back to the kitchen. "How is Matthew's dad doing?"

"Every day brings something new that he needs to deal with, and he's sleeping more and more as they change his medications. He wants to have an assisted death and I think it can't be that far away from what Matthew tells me. He hasn't talked about MAID, but I know it has to be on his mind."

Making A Difference

They talked about any number of things about the imminent death, but Neal only surmised what was happening as Matthew kept his thoughts to himself. The spaghetti was cooked and soon steaming bowls were being delivered to the table with toasted garlic-cheese-bread.

Neal called, "Brock and Matthew, supper is on." He went back to the kitchen and brought out the flowers as a centrepiece. The trouble was that it was too tall to see across the table. Neal moved them to the fireplace mantle.

"Thank you for the beautiful flowers. I think they are just what I needed today. I haven't told Mom, but I think the day is fast approaching for Dad to choose to die." His face crumbled and tears flowed down his face. Neal knelt beside his chair and embraced him until the tears subsided. "Thank you, Neal.".

Matthew picked at his food; it was evident his mind was elsewhere. The others were helpless to do anything to improve his demeanour.

After dinner they played a board game. That seemed to connect to Matthew's competitive side and took his mind off things, at least for a short time. When Brock and Dirk said goodbye, they hugged both and reiterated they would be there for them when they needed anything and made Neal promise to call.

*****

Bonny and Matthew walked into Doug's room, where he was sleeping. His complexion had a grey palour and Bonny went to talk to the nurse. Matthew stayed behind and took a seat next to his father.

As he sat, Matthew pulled his seat closer to the bed and Doug stirred at the noise. He opened his eyes and in a low voice said, "Son, I think the time is drawing near and I need to set the date. Although the pain is being managed, I sleep all the time. That isn't how I want to go out of this world. I'm ordering less medication so I'll be awake, but I also don't want so much pain that I can't talk. I want the next few days to be quality ones before I die. Where's your mother?"

"She went to talk to the nurses. I'll go see what she's doing."

He saw her leaning over the sign-in register and called to her. When she turned around, her eyes were red from crying. "What's the matter, Mom?"

"The nurse just told me your father has chosen his MAID date and the doctor is coming to talk to all of us. I don't know if I'm ready."

Matthew looked at her and saw how the news aged her, "Will we ever be ready, Mom? We need to have this meeting and support him. Can you make it through OK?"

Making A Difference

"I promised myself I would support him, and I'll not let him down. The doctor will be here shortly so let's go sit with your father before he arrives."

Bonny put on as cheery a face as she could muster, and they went back in. Behind her smile, she felt like she would crack at any moment but willed herself to stay composed. They sat and Doug opened his eyes. "Hi Honey, I love you."

Those three words destroyed her internal composure, but she held it together, "I love you too. How are you feeling today?" She meant what she said but faked everything else. She was a wreck.

"I'm not doing well, and I asked the doctor to come talk to us. I want to choose the date." Doug took all his energy to get the words out and closed his eyes again.

Bonny broke but turned to look out the window hoping to buy time before he opened his eyes again. It worked. When she turned back, his eyes struggled to open into slits. "Honey, if you need to choose a date, we'll support you." No sooner had she said that, Dr. O'Mally stepped into the room.

"I overheard the conversation, so you know he has decided to go ahead with MAID. He has chosen Thursday, the day after tomorrow. Do you have any questions?"

Bonny made it look like she was considering if she had questions but what was really going on inside was her repeating over and over *'Don't cry, Don't cry…'* and kept a stoic look on her face. "Where will it happen?"

Doug spoke, "In the sun…" but that's all he could say. He had exhausted his ability to talk in sentences.

Bonny knew what he meant, "You mean like last week when you sat in your wheelchair and soaked up the sun in the window of the common room?"

Doug smiled and nodded.

She looked at the doctor, "Can we make that happen?"

"Yes, but it has to be done at the hospital, because of the organ donations. If we do it at ten in the morning, the sun will be shining in a room that I selected there. I checked the weather forecast just in case. We'll take him by ambulance and roll him into the room which has a large south-facing window overlooking a garden. You can have up to ten people attend if you wish."

"Thank you Dr. O'Mally."

*****

At the hospital, Doug's bed was positioned to get the most sunshine and he was semi sitting up so he could see the garden area and trees. Bonny was next to

Making A Difference

Matthew who was next to Neal. They stood on one side of the bed while the doctor readied himself on the other side. Staff had brought in chairs, but Bonny wanted to stand. Matthew put the chairs in a row behind them in case they had to take a seat quickly. The doctor had inserted an intravenous line that he would use to administer the medication that would put Doug to sleep and then stop his heart.

Doug looked to Bonny and Matthew, "It's time for me to go. I love you both and I'll see you when your time comes." He was exhausted but he was glad he was able to say his rehearsed statement.

Bonny said, "I love you, rest well."

Matthew was crying but managed, "I love you Dad."

As arranged, Doug nodded to Dr. O'Mally, and he activated the process. They watched as Doug's eyes got heavy and closed and held their breath until the doctor pronounced him dead.

Bonny broke down and sobbed while Matthew embraced her and helped get her seated. He clung to her as Doug's body was transported to the organ collection team.

They sat in the empty room until they composed themselves. Neal stood next to them with tear stains on his face, the aftermath of watching people he loved experience such heart-wrenching pain.

Chapter 38

Grant and Brock visited Axel to get a status on the lawsuit. He had a team of twenty helpers collecting and documenting information about potential victims and then doing the research to see if they were part of what they already knew from Father Mike's documentation or if they were undocumented.

"We've registered our lawsuit and we've been given a court date for October 21 of this year. We have a very strong case with rock-solid evidence for about half of the victims who have registered. The remainder will require more work and our team is making great headway."

Grant asked, "What did the lawyers say when we told them we weren't quitting?"

"They didn't say anything much, the same legal gibberish we lawyers use to try and scare people enough that they stop the lawsuit. They were just bluffing."

"Will they come back again with other tactics?"

"They may, but what I expect is they'll try after the suit is launched. Of course, they won't know what evidence we have so they may wait for that. As we've been processing Father O'Hara's documentation, I've been impressed with his thoroughness and the quality of the documents. The majority of what he gave you is from their archives. We need to disclose our evidence to the lawyers for the Church, so we'll be sending a copy of everything we have ready to them. Once they see that, we may have an offer to settle out of court."

Brock asked, "If we settle out of court, does that mean the result won't be made public?"

Axel commented on Brock's thought, "You're probably correct in your assessment but there are ways to work around it. I'd like the reporter to do a follow up story just before we send the documents over. Can you arrange that? I'd like to have the interview done here with you, Grant, so I can guide you on what we could let out."

*****

Carson checked with his editor, and she agreed to do a follow-up story, so Brock arranged a time with his father and Axel. When they met at Axel's office,

Making A Difference

Carson explained the first story was so popular that his editor jumped at the chance for a follow-up. Axel explained, "I think the public would like to know that our documented evidence came from the archives of the Church so if Carson could bring that out, it gives credibility to the lawsuit."

Carson listened and took notes, "I like that angle. I was also thinking I'd ask Grant how he felt with the response from the first article." He looked at Axel, "Can he talk about the number of people who called in and could he explain how they fit into the lawsuit."

Axel liked that Carson was thinking ahead, "We can give a lot of information and talk about the victims whose claims are supported by the documentation. We can also bring out the different levels of evidence if that would help."

"I didn't get a chance to talk about other lawsuits against the Church that happened, but I thought the information might open people's eyes. What do you think?" Carson asked.

Axel agreed, "I think it will make a powerful story from a couple of perspectives. First it will show that his behaviour isn't something new and second, the courts have dealt with it before. I think all of that will form a great foundation and you could top the whole thing off with what Grant feels about what's happening."

Grant chimed in, "The Church would like to shut us down so if we can get as much as possible out there about where we're in this lawsuit, it can't hurt us."

*****

Dirk ended his call, "Mom and Dad are coming to visit on the weekend. They're coming Friday night, so I'd like them to meet your family. Can you call and invite everyone to supper on Saturday night? I guess we'll have an early Family Supper and it'll be here.

Brock contacted his parents and Tom and Mackenzie. When he got off the phone with his sister he revealed, "Tom's parents just told them they were coming Friday night as well, so we'll all be together. This should be interesting."

*****

William and Jean Harrison arrived in time for supper Friday evening and met Brock when he and Dirk took their luggage into the house. In no time, Brock knew they would be friends. During the meal, conversation flowed easily, and Jean proved to be quite inquisitive of who Brock was and where he came from. She found out more about him in that hour-long supper than most of his friends had learned over his lifetime.

They learned they would meet Brock's family at supper the next night. Much to the surprise of Dirk and Brock, Jean brought up the lawsuit.

Brock didn't know how far to go but thought this would be a good time to show he carried no shame, "Yes, Dad started the lawsuit to help all of the victims overcome the damage the abusers inflicted on so many young, innocent people."

After Jean explained she had read the article, she encouraged Brock to explain Grant's situation.

Brock explained how the abuse caused his father to suffer for years and it affected his relationship with the rest of the family, "I didn't know about the abuse growing up, but I always questioned why Dad was so negative and homophobic." Brock explained his coming out and how he was kicked out of the house. He talked about how that felt and at times was overcome with emotion, but he persevered because he knew Dirk's father needed to hear the story. He explained Grant's commitment to therapy and how he revealed his story to others so he could help rid himself of shame and help others. "You'll be able to ask him tomorrow because he doesn't hesitate if it will help anyone."

*****

Brock had a great day with Dirk and his parents showing them around the garden centre and the pavilion, art gallery, the botanical gardens, and the arboretum. The Pine Valley complex was in various stages of completion, but Brock was able to paint such a vivid picture of his vision that the Harrisons thought they could see it in their minds.

Jean surveyed the arboretum and commented, "I'm looking forward to visiting when you have it completed so I can test what I envision it will be to the actual end product. You're a visionary my young man!" She looped her arm through Brock's arm and sauntered away leaving Dirk and Bill with what they were talking about.

Dirk caught up with them and suggested, "We should be heading back to start to prepare for supper. What time are your parents and Mackenzie and Tom coming with his parents?"

Making A Difference

Brock thought a bit, "I think I told them to come for six. I thought we could have drinks and appetizers while we get to know one another. Let's head back."

At home, everyone pitched in. Soon the appetizers were ready, and the meal was well on its way. Brock made rolls in the morning, rising early to make sure they would be cooked before they left for the day.

They cleaned up and at six, Martha and Grant arrived followed by the Remingtons and Mackenzie. Introductions were made and conversation slipped easily into the room between the soft jazz playing in the background.

Tom's mother, Jenna queried, "Who's responsible for the music?"

Not knowing where that question was leading, Dirk was tentative when he answered, "Me, is something wrong? I can change it if you would prefer something else."

She laughed, "Don't be silly, it's perfect. Music at a gathering is one of my pet peeves. Most people play it so loud it interferes with conversation. You have the right music at the right level."

Dirk smiled, "Thank you."

Frederick, Tom's father, sought out Grant, "I read the articles about your lawsuit, you really got a good response, are you pleased?"

Bill overheard the question and turned around to join in waiting for Grant's response, "Mind if I join in, I read the articles as well."

Grant replied, "Please join in Bill. Frederick, to your question, I'm of two minds. I'm pleased people felt comfortable enough to come forward, but I'm not pleased there are so many people who have been abused. For so many years I felt alone, and it took me decades to finally come to terms with it. I thought I was alone but then I read about the lawsuits that were launched in Newfoundland and Labrador. Because of my shame I tried not to connect with the stories, and I avoided anything about abuse. I've completely changed my stance and the lawsuit is my way to help others who didn't think there was any help to be had."

Frederick nodded, "I admire what you're doing. I have a friend who confided in me and for years I was the only one he could talk to. When I read about your lawsuit, I encouraged him to register. I hope it helps him see he isn't alone."

Bill was watching Grant and Frederick talk and when there was a break, he spoke up, "I registered as well."

Grant looked at him, "Were you abused by clergy too?"

"I was, and I couldn't talk to anyone. I kept it to myself until I got drunk one night and in an emotional mess, I told Jean. That was fifteen years ago, and she carried it with me but I needed more. She convinced me to register. It took me three weeks to get the nerve to contact the lawyer, but I did it. Thank you, Grant." Bill was sincere in his thanks.

Frederick spoke what he was thinking, "Bill, your sentiments could be said by many of the victims who registered. I think a door has been opened and this lawsuit will do so much good. The Church can't just hide those predators anymore. Hopefully, this will help them see the damage they've done and make the necessary changes, so it doesn't happen again. I heard the Pope came out with a statement condemning the abuse, but I hope he has done more inside the church to address the problem."

They talked about the issues and when Frederick bowed out to refill his drink, Bill asked, "Grant, would you mind if we could talk. I have so many questions and no one to talk to."

Grant smiled, "Bill, you're not alone. I'll help you in whatever way you need. Are you available tomorrow?"

"Yes, can we meet up somewhere?"

"Let's meet for breakfast. Come to my place and I'll make you my specialty, poached eggs on toast. Do you like?"

Bill's turn to smile, "It's one of my favourites. Can you make a runny yolk?"

"That's the way I like them, runny yolks, cooked whites! Martha is going out for the day at nine so come for nine thirty and we'll discuss anything. I'm an open book."

"Brock drove us by your home today, so I know where to go. Thank you!"

"Everyone come to the table, supper is ready."

They made their way to the table, and they ate a hearty meal while continuing the conversations from before supper.

Chapter 39

Brock drove with Dirk to look over the progress of the park area of Pine Valley. It was a beautiful early June day and they soaked up the sun's warmth as they strolled the finished pathways of the botanical garden. Brock steered their walk over to the events pavilion to see how the gazebo, bridge and plantings were looking. He wanted that area to look its best for the opening night, the night of the celebration for Andrew and Gregory.

Dirk hadn't seen that part of the park area since early spring and stood looking at all that had been completed, "It really has come a long way. Brock, it is beautiful! You must be pleased!"

Brock smiled at the compliment, "I guess you have only heard about all the things that need to be done that I haven't shared how happy I am with what's happened. I'll try to be better at sharing some of the joy that I feel when I see a piece of the park plan being completed. Do you want to do the rest of the park and I can tell you more about what I've planned?"

"I'd love that. Last fall when we toured the arboretum, I was impressed with the trees that were natural to the area that you're incorporating into the grand design. I want to hear about what you think now." Dirk was animated as he spoke.

They linked arms and followed the meandering pathways which demarked a variety of garden spaces that Brock explained by pointing out future areas of specific plantings as if they were already in place. He had memorized the plan and could see the potential in his mind. Dirk was enthralled with Brock's child-like excitement and tried as best he could to see what Brock could see. He stopped, turned to Brock, and commented, "It will be interesting to see this place when it's finished so I can find out how close I've interpreted your vision."

The greenery was new-growth fresh, and, as they walked, birds of all colours, chipmunks, squirrels, deer, and rabbits frolicked through the forest, using the underbrush and tree branches as perches. "When I was a kid, Mom took me see Snow White and the Seven Dwarfs and, in this moment, I feel like Snow White." Brock said and chuckled at how gay some macho people would see that statement.

Making A Difference

Dirk thought about what Brock had said, "It's remarkable. I guess they've gotten used to the workmen being out here on a regular basis that they aren't as timid as when we first came here."

As they neared the arboretum, Dirk became very interested in the trees and asked questions of Brock about which were his favourite, which had to be removed and what he would plant. They also got talking about the memorial plaques that would be purchased and installed as part of the plan. As they walked down one path, Brock pointed out the large oak tree that he pointed out the last two times they walked this area. "That's my favourite. It should be here for many years after we're gone."

At that Dirk knelt and with a ring box in hand, "Brock, I lost my first love and I never thought I'd find love again, but I found you. I love who you are; your good heart, your vision to make this planet a better place, your care for the marginalized, your enthusiasm with life, and your ethics. I love you. Will you marry me?"

Brock stood in stunned silence before snapping back to reality, "Yes Dirk, I will marry you. I love you for who you are and what you stand for. I want to grow old with you."

Dirk took the ring and placed it on Brock's finger, before standing and kissing him. He brought out a second matching ring and gave it to Brock who knelt and placed it on Dirk's finger, "Dirk, I know you want me to be your husband, but I want you to know I want you to be mine."

Dirk expelled a held breath, "Phew! I was hoping you would say yes because if you hadn't, what would I do with this?" He led Brock to the side of the oak tree and pointed to the stone plaque installed at the base, '*June 20, 2025 Brock Matheson agreed to marry Dirk Harrison.*' and looked at Brock as he read it.

"You were pretty sure of yourself. After all, it's now written in stone!" Brock smiled and kissed Dirk again. "You are a wonderful man."

Dirk suggested "Let's keep this a secret until your Sunday family dinner and announce it then."

Brock frowned, "That's two days away, how will I be able to keep from mentioning this to anyone?"

"Get yourself involved in the work that has to be done here and you'll soon get lost in the details. I think it'll be a good thing to tell your parents and your sister all at the same time." Dirk leaned into him and gave him another kiss, "You can do this, I know you can!"

Making A Difference

*****

Mackenzie and Tom were out for a romantic picnic, at least in her mind. They packed a picnic basket and were looking for just the right spot, something quiet but with nice scenery. They rounded the corner to a grassy knoll bordering the lake's edge which presented itself as the ideal place. They laid out the blanket and sat down to start getting the food ready. Once they had their plates full, Mackenzie started talking about how wonderful she felt their relationship was. He agreed as he took another bite of his submarine sandwich.

Feeling a little bit disappointed that Tom wasn't being romantic, she decided to follow through on her plan. She took his hand and told him how much she loved him, how she would like it if he would agree to marry her, and slid a ring on his finger.

Tom almost choked on his sandwich, "Marry you? If you're serious and this is no joke, yes, I would love to marry you!"

"Why would you think it was a joke?"

"Women don't propose."

"This one does. Why does everything always have to be the man's way?"

Tom could see this was heading in a direction he didn't want it to go so he did what he could to put back the romance, "Mackenzie, you have just made me the happiest man. I love you so much and for you to want me to share your life, all I can say is yes, I will marry you."

It worked. Mackenzie softened and drifted into her romantic ideal of a proposal. "I love you, Tom. Here, you can ring me."

He took her hand and uttered loving and romantic sentiments before sliding the ring on her finger, "We're engaged. We can tell your parents tomorrow."

"Yes, let's announce it as soon as we sit down."

*****

Brock and Dirk arrived for Sunday family dinner without their rings on. They planned to make their announcement at the table and agreed to put their rings on just before.

Mackenzie and Tom arrived, greeted everyone with hugs and stood around the kitchen helping with the final touches with dinner. The chatter covered all the regular topics and each person gave updates on their piece of the world. The shelter was operating at full capacity and Tom's workload was keeping him busy. Dirk talked about another app they had developed which was on trial with a select group of users. Brock talked about the park area and the final touches to the event pavilion

Making A Difference

which would be ready for Andrew and Gregory's celebration later in the week. Grant talked about getting the last things done and how he was starting an apartment complex in the South End. Martha talked about the planning her department at the university was going through to get ready for the fall. In no time supper was ready and they each carried dishes into the dining table.

Everyone had served themselves when Brock and Mackenzie spoke at the same time, "We have some news." They both gave puzzled looks to each other, and Brock broke the impasse, "You go first."

"I wanted us to all be together before we shared our news. She took Tom's hand and held it up next to hers. They had complementary rings, "We're engaged! I've always thought it funny that only the female gets a ring so when I proposed, I had two rings."

Tom smiled, "I was planning on proposing but she got to execute her plans before I had a ring. I'd never have thought of two rings."

Mackenzie faux punched his arm, "That's why I needed to smash the old male-oriented norm and create a new, more-equal tradition."

Their parents congratulated them and listened to Mackenzie's views on the ceremony they'll have. Martha commented, "It all sounds exciting. I just know it will be a different version so let me know what has to happen so we can help."

Mackenzie looked at Brock, "Beat that!"

He looked at Dirk and they held up their hands showing matching rings. "We're engaged too!" He lowered their hands and explained their walk in the park area of Pine Valley on Friday, how Dirk proposed in front of his favourite tree and finished with the engraved stone plaque.

His parents congratulated them before Martha looked at Grant, "I guess we have two weddings to prepare for."

They talked about wedding generalities without any specific dates or plans decided when Mackenzie suggested, "Why don't we have a double ceremony? She looked at Tom and then at Brock and Dirk, "What do you think?"

Brock thought for a few seconds, "We haven't discussed anything yet but that's something to consider"

Dirk joined in, "If we can agree on things, I'm all for a double ceremony. I don't want big and flashy, a more comfortable smaller type wedding."

Tom added his views, "I agree with Dirk, I'd like a more casual friends and family event." He looked at Mackenzie, "That's what you were suggesting this past week. You even said you would like to get married outdoors."

Making A Difference

"I think Pine Valley sounds wonderful but what do you want Brock?" Mackenzie put him on the spot.

Brock smiled, "We haven't talked about it but an outdoor ceremony in Pine Valley would be wonderful. I could go for that and then we could have the reception in the pavilion."

They spent the rest of the dinner discussing wedding options and by the time dessert was finished, they had nailed the plans. They would have a double ceremony on October 4th with coloured leaves as their backdrop.

Making A Difference

Chapter 40

Brock used his key to open the doors to the pavilion. He and Dirk walked through the facility and made sure the place was ready for Andrew & Gregory's celebration. Over two hundred guests were attending this evening and a group of friends were coming soon to decorate. As they walked into the main gathering room, they were taken back by the panoramic view that greeted them.

Dirk whistled, "Wow, Brock, this is beautiful. The way the windows are positioned, they look out onto the lake and the colourful plantings showcase the scene."

Brock was pleased with his reaction, "Matthew did such a great job designing this place! I'm beyond happy with the way it turned out."

"I think this will be the hot, new venue for people to hold their receptions."

Brock nodded, "I'm hoping it will be. Charlene, our marketing person, has been booking events out two years and we have a busy agenda already. I wanted Andrew and Gregory's celebration to be our first event and tomorrow we're holding an open house for the public to see it."

Dirk took a quick look, "I hear people."

"I think we're about to start decorating." They went to the entry and helped manage the boxes of decorations Mackenzie and Tom unloaded from his car. More people arrived and before long, the decorating was done.

Brock walked Anson and Charles out with Matthew and Neal. As they went to their cars, he waved goodbye, "I will see you tonight!"

*****

The guests started arriving in all manner of formal attire. Music formed a background as the guests marveled at the panoramic view. People, with drinks in hand, chatted with each other as waiters circulated with finger food. Brock knew that the majority of the guests knew each other so he had a level of comfort that people would connect with whom they wanted.

It was such a joyful moment for Brock when he spotted his dad dressed in a tux walking in with his mom on his arm wearing a silver shimmering flowing gown. They looked like a Hollywood couple walking the red carpet as they greeted this person or that couple with such an air of confidence. He thought back to when he

Making A Difference

came out to them, and they kicked him out of the house. They have evolved so much in a relatively short time and now they run the Pflag Chapter. They walked over to him, and as they stood chatting, he spotted Mackenzie and Tom arrive. She was dressed in an avantgarde off-the-shoulder gown in an emerald-green colour which matched Tom's bow tie. Her prom popped into his memory and how important it was to her that her ex-boyfriend, Ben, have a matching tie, cummerbund, and handkerchief. He thought to himself, *'Some things don't change as much as others.'.*

He announced their arrival to his parents with, "Here comes trouble!" His parents turned to see who he was talking about and saw Mackenzie & Tom make a beeline for the three.

They greeted Mackenzie and Tom and chatted about the hall and their double ceremony in just over three months.

"Where's Dirk?" Mackenzie asked.

"He should be here shortly." Brock said as he watched the door and saw Matthew approaching with Neal on his arm. They were wearing matching black tuxes with accessories in a deep crimson. Matthew wrapped his arms around Brock in a tight hug and when he released him, Neal followed suit. They greeted Brock's family, now standing to one side and engaged in general chatter.

Brock excused himself when Dirk walked in wearing a royal blue tux and looking as handsome as ever. They chatted and Dirk stayed by his side as he greeted more of the guests.

Anson and Charles arrived, chatted a bit and went on their way saying they had to look around the pavilion and headed straight for the glass wall which was becoming renamed as the *'Lake Wall'* because the lake's glass-like surface was shimmering in the evening sun and created quite the spectacle.

More guests arrived and when Jeremy arrived with his mother, he spent several minutes catching up. Henry, Jeremy's ex boyfriend walked up and tapped Jeremy on the shoulder and hugs ensued. He introduced his new boyfriend, Marcus, a doctor in training at the Regional Hospital. Brock reflected as he met the people, he knew this room was a veritable walk down memory lane.

Andrew and Gregory arrived looking very dapper and complimented Brock on the pavilion complex and the view. Andrew spoke first, "You certainly have outdone yourself. This is a magnificent addition to Saint John."

Gregory stepped forward, "Congratulations Brock. Who knew that our gardener who had mud always on his face could clean up so well and achieve so much? This is beautiful! When will the art gallery open?"

Making A Difference

"We have our first art exhibit two weeks from tonight. It will be a selection of the amazing art that talented residents from the homeless shelter have produced. I want to give them a helping hand. It isn't charity because they have talent and potential. I'm hoping a show will give them the confidence to continue."

*****

At the appointed time, the guests took their seats and enjoyed scrumptious food and engaging conversation at their tables.

Brock took his place on the stage and gazed out over the more than two hundred guests finishing their meals. "May I have your attention? Tonight, we have two celebrations. First, we have an anniversary. Twenty years ago today, four couples sat in a courtroom in Moncton awaiting their case against the Province of New Brunswick to be heard. Two of the couples, Jason Harding and Peter Ellsworth and Elizabeth Channing and Cynthia Depoe wanted the province to allow same-gender marriage so they could get married. The other two couples, Victor Rawling and Robert Thibodeau and Andrew Wallace and Gregory Allen had married elsewhere and wanted the province to recognize their marriages. In court that day, they found that the province's lawyer wasn't going to fight the case although all along the papers cited that the province was against same-gender marriage. The lawyer told a different story, and the judge asked the lawyers on both sides to get together and sort it out. They put their heads together and New Brunswick made same-gender marriage legal and within a month, the Government of Canada made same-gender marriages legal. It was a long and difficult battle province by province but because of the perseverance and hard work carried out by people like these eight courageous people in provinces across this great country they were successful. I'd like to have the couples stand up so we can thank them for their contribution to making New Brunswick and Canada a better place to live." As he announced each couple again, they stood to thunderous applause and a standing ovation. As the applause quieted, people started to sit again.

"The second is that Carson Drummond has written a book about Andrew and Gregory's activism for LGBTQ equality. Kaleisha was working for them at Mahogany Manor before she purchased it and overheard the stories that they had been part of in the fight for equality. We spoke about this one day in the kitchen and decided to put their names forward for a Governor General's Order of Canada. Tonight, I want to announce that they'll be travelling to Ottawa in October to receive the Order of Canada for their work with Human Rights." Applause broke

Making A Difference

out while a standing ovation ensued, guests started chanting Andrew and Gregory's names wanting them to speak.

Brock calmed the room down, "Well guys, everyone wants to hear from you. Please come on stage."

They reluctantly made their way to the microphone looking stunned from the news as they tried to compose themselves.

Andrew stepped forward, "Boy, there's nothing like getting blindsided in front of your friends! Never in our wildest dreams did we expect to be awarded for the activism we did. I wish my dad could see this because when I was growing up, he never had anything nice to say about gays let alone think I could be awarded for my gay activities.

It certainly has been a journey. Many times, we got shunned in public or faced pointing and whispering behind hands when we went into a restaurant. We could only imagine what they were saying. At home we received less than cordial phone calls or shots fired at our home and bright graffiti painted on our walls, all because we were gay or that we dared to speak out. We've had stalkers, who blatantly told us we deserved to go to hell, and some people who spread ghastly rumours about us sexually abusing our grandson. The possibility there would be attempts on our lives was ever present in our minds and we wondered if that's what the shots were meant for. Thankfully, we made it through it all and live a relatively boring life today." He looked toward Gregory and after receiving his nod, he moved to the side.

Gregory stepped up to the microphone, "What Andrew said." Everyone laughed. "Seriously, to live true to who we are, we needed a world where being gay was a non-issue. I don't think we're 100% there yet but we've come a long way from when we became a couple. The early years were hard, we figured if anyone knew we were gay, we could lose our families or our jobs or whatever straight people take for granted. The inequity of the two worlds made us mad and when we were forced into coming out, our world became so different. We weren't living in fear anymore but there was a lot of uncertainty. As the uncertainty diminished, we began taking control of our lives. We deemed that if anyone had a problem with us being gay, that was their problem, and we found an internal strength we didn't know we had or even thought possible during our time in the closet. This strength allowed us to decide to start to make a difference in the lives of our LGBTQ community. We started standing up for what we felt was right and didn't back down when the straight world assumed we would. We found our purpose." He saw that Andrew had something else to say so he stepped aside.

Making A Difference

"When we found our purpose, we connected with other LGBT people who had found theirs and together we tackled the issues that were at hand and supported each other in the fight. As I look around this room tonight, I see the LGBTQ activists and our straight allies who, in their own ways helped make things happen. Never in my closet-life did we expect we would be able to marry but we can. Never underestimate the power of following what's right no matter how unpopular you are. We thank Brock and Kaleisha for nominating us, we'll treasure the award. We want to share this with all of the people who helped our fights be successful. No one or two people can effect the change we've seen over the past thirty years, we all made it happen. Thank you." More applause followed the guys to their seats.

Brock took over the microphone, "Thank you Andrew and Gregory." He started the applause and it burst from every corner of the hall. It lasted until they sat in their seats. "For those of you who are interested, Carson has his book about Andrew and Gregory for sale just outside those doors. It's called 'Our Journey to Equality" and ten percent of the profit goes to support the work of Pflag Canada which Andrew and Gregory spent twenty years supporting with their time. This is a celebration and what would a celebration be without dancing. I see the band is ready so get up and dance! Enjoy!"

Making A Difference

Chapter 41

The plans for the double ceremony weddings fell in place and October rolled around faster than either of the couples expected. They tried to keep it small but with family and friends of the bride and three grooms, they settled at 175 who would attend the reception only. Family members were the only ones to be at the actual wedding ceremony. Guests were coming from all over. Honeymoon travel was booked, and each couple would be gone for almost two weeks. Brock and Dirk decided to relax in Puerto Vallarta while Mackenzie and Tom chose to explore Spain. Tom would be moving into Mackenzie's house upon their return.

Brock was the main organizer for the wedding and was happy things were all set for the weekend event. He also had his eye on the court case which was scheduled to start on Tuesday the 21st, just two days after their return. He had wanted to attend the Order of Canada presentation for Andrew and Gregory at the end of the month, but he stepped aside for their family. The kids along with their spouses and children were travelling to Ottawa to see their dads receive their awards. October would be a full and emotionally charged month.

Brock was reviewing his list and calling some of the suppliers to check on delivery. It was a simple ceremony and each of the four getting married chose one person to stand up with them. He had chosen Matthew and Dirk chose his brother, Jack while Tom chose his brother Darren, and Mackenzie chose her best friend, Jill. They chose a lawyer to officiate. Everything was coming together, and he and Dirk were meeting at the Pavilion to check on the food preparations and the table set-up.

They had chosen the arboretum as the place for the wedding. Workmen were putting the finishing touches on the gazebo he had built amongst the trees for the ceremony. Brock felt confident everything was ready for their big day.

*****

The wedding day was upon them and there was a frenzied energy taking over the members of the wedding party. Dirk's family were staying at Dirk's place and were getting ready in their respective suites while he and Brock ignored any superstition and dressed together in their bedroom. Brock had loaned his place to Tom's family and when they returned to Truro on Sunday, Matthew and Neal would start moving in. They had to be out of their Queen Square apartment by the end of the month.

Mackenzie got ready at her home with Jill and Martha, and Grant arrived to take them to the pavilion. Tom picked up his brother at Brock's home and his parents followed them to the site. Dirk's family took their car and followed Brock and Dirk in Dirk's car. Everyone arrived on time and parked their cars for use after the reception. They boarded the rented limousines and travelled in a motorcade to the arboretum. The drive into the gazebo was ablaze with the fall colours which provided a spectacular backdrop for the ceremony. Andrew and Gregory were in charge of the music and once the family members were standing in place, Brock gave them the nod and music filled the air.

The lawyer waited as each couple walked hand-in-hand up the stairs stopping in front and to each side of her. The couples had agreed on the simplicity of the ceremony and that each person would write their vows. The officiant welcomed everyone, and she gave a short introduction. She went through what needed to be said and alternated back and forth between the two couples getting to the saying of the vows. Mackenzie went first with a thought-provoking sentiment that mixed emotion with equality of the sexes. Tom followed with a somewhat simpler statement of love and commitment. The lawyer turned to Dirk for his vow, and he gave a thoughtful and loving statement while Brock's vow expressed his love and hopes for their future. Rings were exchanged and the officiant pronounced them married. She directed them to seal their marriage with a kiss and took them aside to sign the paperwork. When they were finished, they filed back into the centre of the gazebo Mackenzie and Tom were introduced as husband and wife and Brock and Dirk as husband and husband.

Cheers filled the air and the couples spoke to the family members about nerves or some funny thought they had mid ceremony. Andrew and Gregory congratulated the couples and bid them farewell. They headed to the pavilion to ready themselves to greet the guests and make sure things were all set for the wedding party to arrive. As Masters of Ceremony, they reviewed their schedule and waited for the first guests while the wedding party finished up.

Brock had given the photographer a list of the wedding shots they wanted, and he took a variety of pictures. It took a while, but he was able to process them all. The afternoon sun had provided enough warmth that everyone remained comfortable. As the day wore on, a chill started to settle over them and they were glad, when the time came, to be loading into the limousines to be ferried back to the pavilion for the reception.

Making A Difference

*****

Andrew and Gregory had the background music ready and checked out the appetizers and refreshments. As the guests arrived, they were directed to the guest book stations which differentiated the guest books by a large photo of the couple above the book. Guests signed the appropriate guest book and many signed both. They then filtered into the room and found where their seats were located and then indulged in the refreshments and appetizers.

The hall was filling, and the guys turned the music up to provide some escape from the noise as it increased. Brock had arranged that the guests would have arrived before the wedding party by giving them a time fifteen minutes before the wedding party planned to be there. This worked well and when the wedding party arrived, most of the invited guests were present. The families were escorted to their designated places and the parents took their seats at the parents' table. The attendants, Jack, Darren, Matthew, and Jill were seated at the head table. The couples came to the door and an explosion of applause erupted even before they were announced. The guys calmed the room and introduced each couple. They were escorted to the head table where, once they had their seats, each person was introduced.

The food was served, Andrew and Gregory invited the attendants to give speeches. Matthew told a humourous story about Brock and made a point of telling the group, "When we dated, I thought we would marry and here we are but I'm not the groom. Like they say, the best man won. Wait a second. Brock, I'm your Best Man, what gives? Just kidding." The room laughed and he finished with heartfelt wishes for the grooms to have a long life together.

Jill followed with stories of when Mackenzie got on her propensity to soapbox about one issue or another and talked about a time she got confused and gave an emotional plea for gay rights when she should have been talking about climate change.

Jack talked about being the younger brother to Dirk, a brainiac. He recounted the disappointment he caused many a teacher who had expected him to perform in a similar way but soon learned to lower their expectations. He wished Dirk and Brock a long and happy marriage and then threw in that he was about to get his PhD, so he did OK for himself.

Darren also told stories about being brothers with Tom, but he was no brainiac. People chuckled and he went on, talking about adventures they had and the amazing things he learned from Tom. He thanked him and wished him a lifetime of married bliss.

The couples had decided that two cakes were an extravagance that they didn't need so they ordered one large multi-layered cake. For a cake top, they had ordered a floral spray and then on the next layer down, they put two men in tuxedos on one side of the cake and a bride and groom on the other. This way, each couple stood on their respective sides and did the cake-cutting ceremony at the same time. Each couple took pieces of the cake, laid out on platters, and some napkins before visiting each table. They introduced themselves if they didn't know the people or chatted if they did. This way, they got to meet everyone at the reception, and everyone got a personal greeting from each of the couples.

When they finished, the dance was announced. Mackenzie grabbed Tom's hand and ran to the dancefloor. A rousing piece of funky music started playing and they began to move together in wild and funny ways. Without anyone knowing, they had choreographed their first dance and provide quite the entertainment.

Dirk and Brock watched and as people clapped and whistled Dirk looked at Brock "Did you know they were doing that?"

Brock slowly shook his head, "Nope, this is new to me."

"So, how do we top that?"

Brock had an idea and whispered something. Dirk laughed and grabbed Brock's hand. While Mackenzie and Tom were gyrating, bopping, and energetically moving to the music, Brock and Dirk faced each other, bowed at the waist, got into the poise, and began to waltz. The room exploded. Each couple had their first dance.

People began to go up to the couples and said goodbye. The grand escape had begun. Before too long the room emptied leaving the wedding party and a few stragglers to say good night before leaving.

Mackenzie and Tom went to her place to pack as they were leaving for Spain at five in the morning. Dirk and Brock went home to change and spent the night in the Hilton. They took their luggage for Puerto Vallarta with them and planned to leave the car at the airport.

*****

Both couples were on the flight from Saint John to Toronto and, from there, went their separate ways. Their flights were unremarkable and both couples were thrilled with the heat they encountered when they walked off their planes.

Making A Difference

The two weeks went by quickly. Mackenzie and Tom rested the first two days and then decided to sign on to a ten-day bus tour that had had a rigorous schedule of getting up at five or six in the morning, depending on where they were travelling that day. They saw large cities and small villages and in each they got to tour many craft making artisans' studios and ancient historical sites. When they returned to Saint John, they were exhausted, and it took almost a week for them to get over their vacation.

Dirk and Brock mainly relaxed but did take a couple of area land excursions and toured Banderas Bay on a rented yacht for several hours one day. They returned to Saint John well rested.

Chapter 42

Grant listened to the ringing and then the connection, "Brock, Axel called, and they just got back to him on our final counteroffer, and they are accepting. He wants to see us this morning at ten, can you make it? Mackenzie and Martha will be there as well."

"I'll see you there. Why does he want us, isn't it pretty straight forward?"

Grant thought the same thing but there are things they needed to know, "He wants to make sure we understand what we can say and what we can't if people ask about the out-of-court settlement."

"OK, I'll see you there."

*****

The Mathesons sat in the conference room waiting for Axel. When he walked in, he addressed the room, "Sorry about the wait but the Church's lawyers had some last-minute tweaking but nothing that affects what we had agreed to yesterday. This was down to the wire. We would be sitting in court right now if they hadn't agreed to our counteroffer. I'll review the main items. The Catholic Church will give each of the 307 victims a written apology and a monetary payout which cannot be disclosed to anyone outside of the lawsuit. In fact, to receive the money, they each must sign a non-disclosure agreement. All costs are covered, so this means you'll not have to pay any of the legal fees or disbursements. The few predator priests who are still living have pleaded guilty and will be dealt with by the courts. Grant, not only will you need to sign the non-disclosure agreement, but each of your family members will need to as well." He looked at Martha, Brock, and Mackenzie, "The lawyers want to make sure you're aware you have to follow the terms of the agreement. Are there any questions?"

Grant looked a bit perplexed, "How do I respond to the calls from the media? They have been calling me regularly for an update on the lawsuit since Carson's stories were published. My name is out there."

"Here are guidelines about what you can say and what you can't. Axel passed around sheets to each of them, "Basically, you can say that we reached an out-of-court settlement with the Catholic Church, but you cannot disclose the terms of the agreement. From there you can talk about how you feel about it as long as

Making A Difference

you don't disclose any of the specifics. Do the interviews but keep them light and more about your feelings. There will be a news release this morning if it isn't out there already. It will be announcing the out-of-court settlement but not much more. The press will already know by the time you leave this office."

Brock asked, "Since we used the information from other lawsuits which are public as the basis for setting the monetary payout, can we state something to that effect? We wouldn't be stating an amount but that would give people an idea."

"No, please do not deviate from the information on that sheet. Nothing is to be said about the payouts, they are between the church and each individual victim."

Brock looked like he had just been reprimanded. He sat back and concentrated on his sheet of paper.

Martha finally spoke, "I'm glad this is over, and the victims will get some money, not that any amount of money will repay any of them for the damage the priests did. I am also glad, as you know, that the victims do not have to get on the stand and relive their abuse. That was always my stumbling block."

Grant's phone sounded. He looked to the others and answered. He spoke for several minutes and hung up. "That was Carson, and he will be interviewing me before lunch at our home."

Axel gave a little shake to his head, "And so it starts. Good luck and keep those talking points close."

*****

Carson met with Grant and got his story. Before he left, he asked Grant's permission and contacted a news reporter for the local BTV affiliate. While on the phone, he passed it to Grant and through the conversation he could tell the news story for TV would happen shortly.

Carson took his phone back when the call was ended, "This is big news and I expect it will be on the evening news tonight. I'll be watching to see what they bring out."

Grant looked at him, "No more than you got, I do have that non-disclosure agreement."

"No, I mean I'd like to see what they put with your interview. I'll bet they'll be using footage from past cases as a backdrop." Carson explained.

"As long as they don't make it look like I said anything I shouldn't have said."

Making A Difference

*****

Brock answered his phone, "Andrew, aren't you about to receive your award?"

"Yes, they are about to file us into the chamber, but I had to call to tell you how much it meant to me that you and Kaleisha did this for us. When we did the activism we did, it wasn't for any glory. We wanted LGBT people to have better, more equal lives and now, the government we took to task is bestowing one of the top awards this country gives its citizens. The absurdity of that hit me just a few minutes ago."

"Do your kids realize the meaning of the award you're getting?"

"I really didn't know until I overheard my grandson ask my daughter what it all meant. Her answer brought tears to my eyes. All along I thought they didn't understand the sacrifice we made for others, but I was wrong. She spelled out everything. They know. After she explained it to him, he came running over and congratulated Gregory and me and said we were all going out to supper to celebrate. It makes me so proud that my kids are proud."

"I'm so happy to hear this. Dad's court case has settled out of court. I'll tell you more when you get home."

"Great news, Brock! I'll get your details later but right now; Gregory wants to talk for a minute. I'll sign off, I love you!"

Gregory's voice came on the line, "Thank you Brock. It has all become so real to us since we arrived. The Kids really understand. I can't tell you what this means to us. Oh, they're moving us, we have to go, Love you!"

"Love you guys too! Have a wonderful celebration!" Brock ended the call.

*****

Kaleisha was scurrying around the kitchen, tidying up and, putting things away, "Roger, I want to catch the news at five. Andrew and Gregory received the Order of Canadas this afternoon and I expect there will be a story about them. All our guests are in, so I'll be able to relax if you promise me, you'll look after anyone who needs something. I really want to watch the news without any interruptions?"

Roger went over to her and embraced her, "Of course I will Sweetie, I know how important this is to you. If it wasn't for you and Brock, they may not be receiving the awards."

Making A Difference

The phone rang and when Kaleisha answered it, she heard Brock's voice, "Hey Kaleisha, are you going to watch the news to catch the Governor General's awards?"

"We were just talking about that, and my wonderful husband is going to make sure I get to see the whole thing without interruptions. I'm all excited!"

"I can tell. Anyway, I was talking with Andrew, and he was thanking us both for nominating them. I've never heard them so excited. I guess it's just that kind of day."

She remembered that he had just gotten back from his honeymoon, and she asked about their vacation. He filled her in and then told her about the out-of-court settlement for his father's lawsuit. He told her that Grant had been interviewed for a news story on BTV so for her to be on the lookout.

*****

The news came on and they mentioned the awards and the lawsuit, so Kaleisha knew both stories were coming on as local news. Roger sat next to her and was very quiet, so he didn't disturb her. He could hear the doorbell and had a phone with him hoping neither would sound until the news was over.

He started to ask something when Kaleisha saw Andrew and Gregory's picture, "Ssshhh, this is the story,"

The newscaster was introducing the story, "This next story is about two men who have been active over the past thirty years fighting for equality for LGBTQ people. Andrew Wallace and Gregory Allen have received the prestigious Governor General's Order of Canada for their contribution to Human Rights equality. Here is some file footage of them over the years." Several pieces of old footage showed the guys at different ages fighting for one issue or another. Kaleisha smiled as she saw her friends younger and thinner with no grey hair. Then they switched over to the ceremony that afternoon from Ottawa and the voiceover told, about them receiving the awards.

The newscaster summarized, "These two men gave of themselves to make a difference in so many lives."

Kaleisha looked at Roger with tears in her eyes, "I'm so proud of them and so pleased to call them my friends!"

Roger reminded her of something she told him, "Remember you said that when you came here you were homophobic. Look at you now proud of your friends who happen to be two gay men. Will wonders ever cease?" He chuckled as Kaleisha swatted him across his shoulder.

Making A Difference

"You stop that. Yes, I was homophobic but that was years ago. I've grown older and much wiser since I moved to Canada."

The newscaster was back, "In this next segment, we have a widely broadcast lawsuit against the Catholic Church by victims who were abused by clergy when they were young. Grant Matheson, a Saint John, New Brunswick man launched the lawsuit, here is his story." The screen filled with Grant sitting in his living room with his wife, Martha. He told his story of abuse and how he confronted his abuser. He talked about the hurt and shame he suffered and how it affected his life and his family. He talked about how the therapy helped him and how the love and support of his family were the main reason he put it behind him. The interviewer asked what made him launch the lawsuit. He explained getting the documentation from Father Mike and how he had his family help him decide what he should do, drop it and do nothing or take the Catholic Church to task. He chose the latter with hesitation from Martha. The interviewer asked why she hesitated. She explained seeing the pain and suffering Grant had gone through and worried about the victims having to relive the abuse when they had to testify in court. She said she was glad the Church settled out of court. The news story talked about other cases but didn't link those cases to Grant's case but did bring out that 307 victims had registered according to the widely read newspaper stories about the suit.

Interviewer, "In earlier news, you said that 307 victims registered. Was that the final number?"

Grant replied, "As part of the non-disclosure agreement, I'm not at liberty to discuss any of the details of the case."

"I understand that, and I apologize for my last question. Can you tell me how you feel about the lawsuit being settled out of court?"

"I wouldn't have agreed to the settlement if I wasn't happy. As Martha said, the victims who bravely came forward and registered wouldn't have to testify and for that, I am thankful. There is a lot of stress with any lawsuit and having it over with has removed all of the stress, other than these interviews but those will be short lived. My family and I have put a lot of effort into the lawsuit and that effort has been rewarded. It's over."

The interviewer summed it up, "Thank you Mr. Matheson. Whether you recognize it, you have made a difference in many lives."

Making A Difference

Making A Difference

Acknowledgments

I have had tremendous support for this, my fourth book in my Journeys of Courage series.

I am forever grateful for the loyalty and commitment of my husband, Ross Leavitt. He has been my constant life supporter throughout our relationship, and he is my first go-to for almost anything I need to do, including this series. He was especially there for me from the first formative ideas to the series' completion and encouraged me every step of the way. Our morning walks proved to be the perfect opportunity to bounce ideas around and many of those ideas helped define the end story line. As part of my editing team, I counted on his attention to detail to identify the issues that I regularly overlook.

I have some of the most intelligent, compassionate, and dedicated friends who contributed to this series in ways some of them may never know, but they were an integral part of making this series come together. I hoist the spotlight on four of those friends who stand out in their contribution:

- ◆ May Matheson-Thomas for her friendship, perseverance, and commitment to editing this story. We talked almost daily for hours some days and out of those conversations, our friendship grew, and the series came together.

- ◆ D.S. Mack MacKenzie for his unending loyalty, his involvement in helping wherever he could, his encouragement, and his seemingly unending stream of creative ideas for getting this series out to the public.

Making A Difference

www.ingramcontent.com/pod-product-compliance
Lightning Source LLC
Chambersburg PA
CBHW011957090526
44590CB00023B/3761